ALSO BY ASSOTTO SAINT

AS AUTHOR

Triple Trouble
(GMP, London, 1987)

Stations
(Galiens Press, 1989)

Wishing For Wings
(Galiens Press, 1994)

*Spells of A Voodoo Doll: The Poems, Fiction, Essays and Plays
of Assotto Saint*
(Richard Kasak Books, 1996)

AS EDITOR

The Road Before Us: 100 Gay Black Poets
(Galiens Press, 1991)

Here To Dare: 10 Gay Black Poets
(Galiens Press, 1992)

Milking Black Bull: 11 Gay Black Poets
(Vega Press, 1995)

Sacred
Spells

Assotto Saint

Sacred Spells

Collected Works

Edited by Michele Karlsberg

Nightboat Books
New York

Copyright © 2023 by Michele Karlsberg
Foreword Copyright © 2023 by Pamela Sneed
Introduction Copyright © 2023 by Jaime Shearn Coan
Editor's Note Copyright © 2023 by Michele Karlsberg

ISBN: 978-1-64362-156-2

Some of the writings in this collection were previously published in such books and anthologies as *In The Life: A Black Gay Anthology* (Alyson Books, 1986), *Tongues Untied* (Gay Men's Press, London, 1987), *New Men, New Minds* (Crossing Press, 1987) *Other Countries: Black Gay Voices* (Other Countries Collective, 1988), *Gay and Lesbian Poetry in Our Time* (St. Martin's Press, 1988), *Stations* (Galiens Press, 1989), *The Road Before Us: 101 Black Gay Poets* (Galiens Press, 1991), *Brother to Brother* (Alyson Publications, 1991), *Sojourner: Black Gay Voices in the Age of AIDS* (Other Countries Press, 1993), *Wishing for Wings* (Galiens Press, 1994), *Jugular Defences: An AIDS Anthology* (Oscars Press, London, 1994), *The Name of Love: Classic Gay Love Poems* (St. Martin's Press, 1995), *Spells of a Voodoo Doll* (Richard Kasak Books, 1996), *The Butterfly's Way: Voices from the Haitian Dyaspora in the United States* (Soho Press, 2001), *Beyond Shame: Reclaiming the Abandoned History of Radical Gay Sexuality* (Beacon Press, 2004), *Freedom in This Village: Twenty-Five Years of Black Gay Men's Writing* (Carroll and Graf, 2005), *Our Caribbean: A Gathering of Lesbian and Gay Writing from the Antilles* (Duke University Press, 2008), *Persistent Voices: Poetry by Writers lost to AIDS* (Alyson Books, 2010) *Indivisble: Poems for Social Justice* (Norwood House, 2013), *Nepantla: An Anthology Dedicated to Queer Poets of Color* (Nightboat Books, 2018) and in such magazines and periodicals as *New York Native Amethyst, Changing Men and The Pyramid Poetry Periodical, Brooklyn Review, QW, Changing Men, Christopher Street, Guys, Outweek, The Portable Lower East Side, PWA Coalition Newsline, RFD, The James White Review, Bay Windows,* and *Vital Signs.*

Photo used for cover art: Rotimi Fani-Kayode

Design and typesetting by Rissa Hochberger and Kit Schluter
Typeset in Egyptienne and Protokoll

Cataloging-in-publication data is available from the Library of Congress

Nightboat Books
New York
www.nightboat.org

Contents

"I can move, move, move any mountain."

—The Shamen

Still
Pamela Sneed

In my mind's eye, the Haitian-born, American poet, playwright, performance artist, publisher, musician, and AIDS activist Assotto Saint was a towering figure. Perhaps because they[1] were in fact over six feet tall. Though they passed away in 1994 of AIDS-related complications, the last time I recall seeing them was in 1992 at the funeral of poet Donald Woods. On that day, Assotto wore high heels and a men's suit. I also recall I first saw Assotto perform sometime in the late 1980s, when they delivered a performance about HIV testing while standing on a table top at the Gay and Lesbian Community Center on 13th Street. For those seated witnesses, Saint appeared gigantic, larger than life. *Sacred Spells* is the work of a gay Black poet who indeed possessed a giant mind, talent, heart, and ferocity. People *still* talk about Assotto, often, everyday, *still*: those young people researching the archive; the Black LGBTQI historians, poets, performance artists, dancers, and friends who knew him; the young Black queers searching for themselves amongst books in the library. When I say *still*, I also mean that when we think of that time in the late 1980s–early 1990s, when the AIDS pandemic raged as the COVID pandemic rages now in the US and across the globe; when we remember the casualties, the terrible losses, the gross homophobia, racism, and crimes against humanity enacted by our government against queer and trans people; when we think of the beacons, the self-ordained priests who carried

1. For the most part I am using him as Saint's chosen pronoun but I also knew them as gender expansive so in current terms I also use they/them.

us through that time, we often think and speak of Assotto Saint.

Indulge me, but if this essay were like a Faith Ringgold painting/quilt with the Statue of Liberty looming large amid some sort of contemporary Middle Passage with Black bodies adrift in the water, you would very pointedly see the crown of Assotto Saint's head floating above. *Crown* is an apt word because Assotto was a king, queen, prince, princess— all members of the royal family combined. They challenged gender binaries; wore makeup, earrings, and dashikis. In poetry and activism they also led. In this compilation, their poems, stories, and plays *still* point us toward a future where queer people of every color have human rights; where healthcare is attainable, accessible for all, and upholds human dignity; where queer people are allowed to exist and present in all our complications and nuances; where we are safe and do not have to hide.

As someone who was a comrade of Assotto, came of age in the early part of the AIDS era, and found my voice amongst so many Black gay men, lesbians and LGBTQI people, I am thrilled and grateful for this compilation of their work. I am struck not only by the tremendous craft and beauty of Assotto's poems, but also by Assotto's insistence to write and speak when they themself, their life partner Jan, and so many around them were dying; to insist upon sex, intimacy, the erotic, and love; to continuously speak truth to power; to fight and rage against the many silences enacted upon Black gay men. I marvel at how so much of the work is an intimate and personal love letter to Jan, to all the lovers and friends they encountered, to all those who fought AIDS. Assotto was someone who, even when riddled with illness, would not back down. They continued to rally and rail against this government's stupidity, inaction, and violence. Reading this work, I am reignited with courage.

On a personal note, as many know (and as I've often spoken and written of), I owe a great deal to Assotto. Maybe we all do. As I've stated, I was there in the church that day in 1992 at the funeral of Donald Woods. I was one of many attendees from Donald's activist family. I was one of many who read the program and saw the glaring omission of Donald's poetry and activist work. The program also stated Donald had died of heart failure. I was one of many who witnessed Assotto speed down the aisle and take over the pulpit mid-service, declaring, "Donald Woods did not die of heart failure; he died of AIDS and he was a proud Black gay man. If you agree with me, stand up." Half the church stood. Half didn't. I stood up, as did Donald's sister, Yvonne. I count that moment as one of a few where my path as an artist was revealed to me.

The second most defining moment in my life happened in 1990, when I attended the "I Am Your Sister Conference" in Boston, a celebration of the work of Audre Lorde. In her first appearance on stage, the self-described one-breasted warrior poet Audre emerged, spread open the arms of her dashiki, and told a crowded room of followers of her battle with cancer. She said, "I began on this journey as a coward." Witnessing the courage of Assotto and Audre shaped me as a poet, a person, teacher, performer. I want everyone I encounter to experience that sense of exhilaration and freedom when the truth is told bare-naked, and to feel the power of standing up for their lives at whatever cost.

Recently, I helped lead a Last Address Tribute Walk in Harlem with several organizations and individuals (the walk was originally developed by Alex Fialho). We went to Harlem at my insistence. In tribute, we went to the addresses of Black gay men who died of AIDS. We went to the address of Bert Michael Hunter who was part of the Black gay writers group Other Countries, and of which Assotto was also a charter member. Donald Woods, Colin Robinson, and Essex Hemphill, among others, were members as well. At Hunter's address, the filmmaker and writer Robert E. Penn and the writer, archivist, and activist Sur Rodney Sur spoke of Bert and belonging to Other Countries. Sur recalled a story of running into Assotto in the late '80s, when Assotto urged him to join Other Countries. They said, "Sur, don't abandon your brothers." I think that statement encapsulates Assotto and what their convictions were.

The title of this collection, *Sacred Spells*, very much refers to Assotto's powerful Haitian ancestry. I was thrilled to learn here that the person born Yves Lubin renamed themself "Assotto," after a drum used in vodoun, and "Saint" after the great Haitian revolutionary fighter Toussaint L'Ouverture. "Saint" also embodies their queerness, claiming self-ownership as a poet and magician whose language conjures, casts spells, and offers protection and healing. No name could be more fitting,

I know in certain Latinx ceremonies, they call the names of the dead and fallen warriors, and the crowd responds "*presente*," to mean *present*.

Assotto's work speaks to us throughout time.

I imagine in the Black Baptist tradition, where I'm from, Assotto's name is called out and with all of my heart and conviction I yell back "PRESENT" to say, he is here, always among us.

Introduction
Jaime Shearn Coan

"i am not going to be upheld by a freak anymore &
i should not be here, screaming out my values when
they happen to be human values/ so what are you
going to do with all this loving energy? i ain't looking
at nobody else but you/"

—Assotto Saint, *Risin' to the Love We Need*

I first encountered Assotto Saint's work in Joseph
Beam's groundbreaking 1986 anthology, *In the Life: A
Black Gay Anthology*, reprinted in 2008 by Redbone
Press. It was an excerpt from his play, *Risin' to the
Love We Need*, where the narrator, Miss Thing (later
to be named Francine), a self-described street queen,
loosely based on the real-life Marsha P. Johnson,
delivers a rousing speech directed at the audience.
Even from the page—even across a time lag of nearly
forty years, I felt the energy of that direct challenge.
That direct challenge led me to seek out more of
Saint's writings, as well as to seek out audiovisual
records of his performances. This led me to Saint's
archive at the Schomburg Center for Research in
Black Culture,[2] to conducting an oral history project, to completing a dissertation, to beginning a book
manuscript, to where I am now, writing to you.

2. Saint's papers are
part of the In the
Life Archive (ITLA), a
collection housed at
the Schomburg Center,
founded by archivist
Steven G. Fullwood
in 1999, dedicated to
preserving the work
of LGBTQ people of
African descent.

This collection of Saint's writings brings
together works that circulated on stages and
pages in the 1980s and 1990s. These words have
been sung, chanted, and recited—activated by
bodies including and exceeding Saint's. Collected
here in this book, they function as an archive.

Saint put together this archive as he was dying, in 1994, assisted by his friend and literary executor, Michele Karlsberg. Karlsberg dedicated herself to finding a publisher for the book after Saint's passing. This collection includes whole manuscripts, as well as pieces published in magazines, literary journals, anthologies, and unpublished writings.

This is an extraordinary legacy. And yet, these pages can only show us glimmers and shadows of Saint's glamor, elegance, poise, precision, timing—in short, his (a)liveness. These pages point to Saint's death as much as to his life. Saint did not take refuge in the belief that he would be reunited with his partner Jan Holmgren in an afterlife. He took the very practical and material action of meticulously planning both of their funerals, buying a shared cemetery plot, and commissioning a tombstone for the both of them. Saint inscribed "Nuclear Lovers" on the tombstone, after a poem he'd written, a clear example of the intertextuality that exists across all of his creations. I don't want to compare this book to a graveyard, but I think it comes out of a similar impulse for something lasting, something tangible, in the face of death. Many of the works in this book refer to death and dying, chronicle the death of people in Saint's orbit, and the deaths of places and cultural practices due to HIV/AIDS. But they also chronicle resilience, celebrate desire, and gesture towards collective healing and health.

What does it mean for us to receive these pieces now? To receive the book as an archive and yet not as an impenetrable text. To receive it as a beginning, as a sourcebook from which to gather strength, to fuel new possibilities, new ways of being—as well as new plays, new poems, new genres. Can we read these works as versions, as the final performance that Saint chose for them? Saint's performances were spaces of transformation. Can this book be one as well?

This book is partially organized (again, by Saint) into separate sections by genre. But this differentiation is a bit deceptive. You won't find a total allegiance to genre here—or in the work overall. That so many genres are included here makes sense for a person who occupied many identity positions. Saint's friend and collaborator George Bellinger, Jr. put it this way:

> He was an amazing guy. He loved the community. And he did not take tea for the fever. He was not gonna erase the fact of his male and female sides, he wasn't gonna erase the fact of his Haitian side, he wasn't gonna erase the fact of being positive and having AIDS, he wasn't gonna erase the artistic side, he wasn't gonna erase the people of color side—when he came in, you had to accept all those sides of him.[3]

Deeply committed to literary initiatives that centered Black gay men and people of color, Saint was a founding member of the Blackheart Collective, and later co-founded the Other Countries writing workshop, publishing in their journals and serving in an editorial capacity.[4] Saint also published in anthologies including *In the Life*, *Brother to Brother*, and *Tongues Untied*. He went on to found Galiens Press in order to edit and publish two of his own anthologies, *The Road Before Us: 100 Black Gay Poets* (1991) and *Here to Dare: 10 Black Gay Poets* (1992), in addition to two collections of his own work, *Stations*

3. George Bellinger, Jr., Interview by the author, April 9, 2019, New York, NY. 73 mins.
4. See Kevin McGruder's concise history of this era: "To be Heard in Print: Black Gay Writers in 1980s New York."

(1989) and *Wishing for Wings* (1994). Saint drew inspiration for these literary initiatives from Black feminist and women of color feminist anthologies, collectives, and presses like Kitchen Table Press. This "for us, by us" or FUBU, approach to publishing likely later extended to his project of developing Metamorphosis Theater with his partner Jan in order to get his theatrical work produced. I want to make visible these collective structures because they hold this book together as well.

Saint was participating in a cultural moment where poetry was often performed—set to music, and sometimes choreography—so there is less of a distinction between poetry and his plays (or song lyrics) than we might think. An embrace of Africanist aesthetics is certainly also at play here, in which story, music, and dance are often inseparable. For the most part, Saint's poems are short lyrics. Bits of conversations, names of people and places, explicit descriptions of sexual encounters, love songs, elegies, outrage—this is some of what you'll find. There are also longer sequences, hybrid pieces (which we might now name lyric essays or prose poems), and performance texts. Perhaps most formally innovative is Saint's series, "No More Metaphors," a three-part prose piece that includes two obituaries and a transcript of a court deposition arising from Saint's arrest at an AIDS action in DC. The series strips away the seeming artifice of the literary device and demands that things be spoken plainly, that material reality be evidenced. By inserting these life records into his literary works, Saint gives form to the radical rupture that took place across all aspects of life with the onset of AIDS and the subsequent neglect by the state to name it and fight it.

With the uncollected poems, we get the pleasure of Saint in process—and are reminded that while some of his works might be finished, his body of work will always be in progress. In "The Language of Dust," Saint alludes to his own imminent death as he sits in front of the double headstone under which his partner is buried: "I will rest / not soon enough / right here / above you / in the shadow / of the trade center / towering / in the distance." Saint died at age thirty-six. Let us take a moment to imagine all the volumes that might have been.

The inclusion of "Uncollected Song Lyrics" is another place where we can see Assotto's editorial hand—or better yet, his hand and his wrist, which was always adorned with his studded leather cuff—a demonstration of his desire to have this performance work archived here as well. Saint's band Xotica, described variously as a "gay new-wave band" and a "rock-theater dance band," was cocreated with his partner Jan and featured his friend and collaborator Willie C. Barnes, and others. They performed "Galiens," "The ACT UP Song," and "Forever Gay" in outlandish outfits, at gay pride events, in clubs, and in theater spaces.

Saint had a full-time administrative job working for New York City Health and Hospitals Corporation. In interviews, he remarked that he wrote poems because they didn't take very long to write. All of the pieces labeled "Fiction" appear in his plays as well, pretty much verbatim—I'm curious about what came first. All in all, Saint's approach to genre could variously be described as revision or adaptation. To say it simply: texts appear and reappear in different forms throughout this collection. Poems show up in plays, works of short fiction do too. But who is to say what form is the original, and does it matter? What do these works *do*, with whom do they associate, in their chosen genres? And what effect is had on us, the reader, as we encounter these iterations across the landscape of this book? Personally, I celebrate the return, the echoes, in Saint's texts, in much the same way that I celebrate the ways in which Saint inserts life records into the realm of the literary.

The essays included in *Sacred Spells* show Saint in his polemical, political, outspoken glory. They also show his attentiveness to current events on an international level, as they impacted members of the African diaspora. For instance, "Why Winnie Mandela Should Go to Jail," published in *Christopher Street* in June 1991, addresses the 1990 trial in which the wife of South African President Nelson Mandela was charged with kidnappings motivated by what Saint calls "homo-AIDS-phobia," and goes on to question issues of Black nationalism and solidarity. Likewise, "A Match with Ashe," published in *QW* in 1992, responds to the media attention placed on the HIV-positive Black tennis star Arthur Ashe, and engages with the topic of outing. In "Haiti: A Memory Journey," first published in the *New York Native* in 1986, and later anthologized, with substantial revisions, in anthologies edited by Edwidge Danticat and Thomas Glave,[5] Saint narrates his early years in Haiti. He does so not just as a nostalgic exercise, but as an antidote to the xenophobic sentiment fueled by AIDS-phobia in the US, which called into question the humanity of Haitians. Writing presumably about himself as well as his nation of origin, he writes: "Haunted by the future, I'm desperate to bear witness and settle accounts." "Sacred Life: Art & AIDS" is the outlier among the essays. It's not a conventional essay; rather, with its fragmentary and

5. Edwidge Danticat, *The Butterfly's Way: Voices from the Haitian Dyaspora in the United States* (2001); Thomas Glave, *Our Caribbean: A Gathering of Lesbian and Gay Writing from the Antilles* (2008).

nonlinear structure, it reads more like a lyric essay. This is another place where we see Saint collapsing the boundaries of genre, gesturing towards the lyric intimacy of his writing and world-making.

The inclusion of Saint's plays (or "theater pieces," as he referred to them) in *Sacred Spells* show Saint's wish for them to remain as dramatic literature. And we are fortunate to have them as such. If you listen closely, you'll find that these plays, on the page, also express an ache, a desire for expression, for embodiment. You might sense the presence of other embodiments in your experience—a feeling that one of Saint's characters describes as "ghosts coming up in my cum."

The plays collected here don't necessarily reflect what occurred onstage during Saint's lifetime. But they do reflect the shape that he ultimately found for them on the page. The scripts were changing things. I want to share with you a little bit of what I know about how these plays happened, because these plays are not just textual objects, they are connected to events that happened in a shared space and time.

As with his literary initiatives, Saint's founding of the Metamorphosis Theater and his theater work in general created the conditions for a range of Black gay male experience to be staged, often for the first time. One of the actors in *New Love Song*, McKinley Winston, said: "I was scared to *death*.... I had never seen a Black gay play prior to the one that I was in."[6] We can hear an echo of Audre Lorde's "poetry is not a luxury" in Saint's description of his plays as "necessary theater." Saint's plays exist within a lineage of Black feminist cultural production. Through his plays, we see Saint carrying forward the legacy of the Black women who influenced him aesthetically

6. McKinley Winston quoted in George Bellinger, Jr., McKinley Winston, Yvans Jourdain, and Issa Jelani group interview by the author, November 10, 2018, New York, NY. 60 mins.

and politically, particularly Marsha P. Johnson, Josephine Baker, Florynce "Flo" Kennedy, Audre Lorde, and Ntozake Shange.

Risin' to the Love We Need features an intergenerational group of Black gay men and a Black trans woman[7] outside the Christopher Street Piers on June 28th, 1980, the anniversary of the Stonewall Riots. In a series of vignettes interspersed with dialogue, song, dance, and ritual, the characters share aspects of their histories and explore their relationships to each other and to white gay culture. Saint draws explicit ties between struggles for Black self-determination and Stonewall, and places his characters' lives in the context of world events. *Black Fag*, a solo performance piece that Saint performed in the Lower East Side club 8BC in 1984, primarily takes place at the Mineshaft, a gay leather bar in the Meatpacking District. It opens with Saint in a "cruising costume" of black sneakers, jeans, and a T-shirt, walking through the audience, passing out masks as he says: "Here I am with a thousand shadows of myself." Saint's 1989 play *New Love Song* offered stories, dancing, rituals, and chants derived from the African-diasporic practices and belief systems of Vodou, Santería, and Yoruba. Saint and his cast addressed the stigma of being marked as Haitian, Black, gay, and HIV-positive, and demonstrated the strength to be found at that intersection instead.

New Love Song took place alongside other works of theater and performance that directly addressed AIDS, mostly coming out of New York City. Among the most well-known, of course, are Larry Kramer's *Normal Heart* (1985) and Tony Kushner's *Angels in America: A Gay Fantasia on National Themes* (1991). In the realm of dance, works by Bill T. Jones and Neil Greenberg addressed AIDS in radically

7. Note on terminology: the character of Francine is referred to as both a "street queen" and "drag queen" in the play—labels which were contemporary to the period. Discussing the character in the language of the present, "trans woman" or "transgender woman" feels more appropriate to me.

different ways. In the lesser-known realm of experimental theater, I would place Saint's work in proximity to theater productions by the Iranian-born Reza Abdoh, and the creation, by choreographer Ishmael Houston-Jones, musician Chris Cochrane, and writer Dennis Cooper, of *THEM*, which premiered in 1986. The West Coast performance troupe Pomo Afro Homos perhaps came the closest to sharing Saint's intention of staging contemporary Black gay male life in all its complexity.

The factors of Saint's early death, his choice of working in an ephemeral medium, and a lack of fiscal support—no doubt connected to his emphasis on centering Black gay male life—have all contributed to less awareness of Saint's theatrical work. Black theater and performance is currently enjoying more visibility, thanks in no small part to sustained pressure placed on white institutions. We see this in the recent Broadway restaging of *For Colored Girls...* and Michael R. Jackson's Tony Award-winning musical *A Strange Loop*. As I watched both of these productions recently, I conjured Saint's presence—what would he make of this, I wondered? It's a bittersweet victory, to be sure.

*

Why was it important for Saint, as his death approached, to know that this collection would be stewarded into publication? Saint cared about his legacy, absolutely. He also cared about the legacy of his peers—the people he knew and loved, and the larger movement of Black gay male writers and cultural producers that was under threat of erasure by HIV/AIDS and white supremacy. In a 1993 interview, Saint said: "There will be a tremendous amount of loss, but I don't see the Black gay writers' community dying. Yes, many of us are going to die. But there's a new generation coming up, and I'm not pessimistic."[8]

The hunger for Saint's texts—from the new generation(s), from his peers, is clear in the demand for the increasingly rare copies of the out-of-print collection that was published in 1994. This publication has the capability of re-establishing genealogical throughlines. But I ask you: Can we hold the sacredness of the page and allow breath to pass through it? Can we hold both the fixity and flexibility of these texts? Can we sense the other versions and the happenings that ghost them? Something is printed on the page. *And also*, other instances, other instantiations, have, and will, exist.

Saint was very out about living with AIDS. In his electric appearance in Marlon Riggs' 1993 documentary film *No Regret (Je Ne Regrette Rien)*, he catalogues a number of the spaces he has cruised for sex over his lifetime. He then looks straight into the camera and declares, "I've done it all, and I regret *nothing*." His refusal to associate any aspect of his life with shame served as a model for those around him as well as for us who follow.

Saint was deeply enmeshed in the spaces in which he created these works. He wrote side by side in writing groups, he wrote at the piers, he recited his poems in the middle of the night, walking around his neighborhood of Chelsea. Saint honored the people and places around him who enabled his survival. He brought their names into his poems, he brought their stories into his plays. He dedicated poems, plays, performances, readings, and books to his loved ones, both living and lost.

He dedicated *Sacred Spells* to you, to *nobody else but you.*

8. Liz Galst, "Silent Scream: AIDS is Quietly Devastating the Black Gay Arts Community." *The Boston Phoenix*, February 19, 1993. Assotto Saint Papers, Box 25, Folder 11, Schomburg Center for Research in Black Culture, New York, NY.

Call His Name
Michele Karlsberg

Assotto was many things, but above all he would say, "I am a Poet." Assotto Saint (Yves François Lubin) was indefatigable. Diagnosed with HIV in November 1987, he immediately started to prioritize because he knew time was of the essence.

In 1990, at the Outwrite conference in San Francisco, Assotto approached me after I spoke on a panel and asked if I would like to work with him at Galiens Press. As soon as we arrived back to New York City, his home became my second home, and we began our working relationship. We immediately formed a sibling bond. He said he felt protected. I knew this was a special tie. I was especially honored to be the person chosen to help make all of Assotto's publishing dreams come true. With a shared focus and strong belief in the work, we forged on, planning the future of Galiens Press. Assotto stayed as focused on editorial as I did on production, distribution and publicity. He thanked me for being his encouraging big sister. I cherished every moment of our life and labors together.

I spent a lot of time with Assotto and his partner Jan in their apartment on West 22nd Street in New York City, a comfortable second-floor apartment with a terrace overlooking 8th Avenue. A small desk sat right outside the kitchen and from there, with his beloved word processor, Assotto worked day in and day out. This space was not only his home, but a creative workspace.

Assotto started Galiens Press in 1988 and self-published his collection of poetry, *Stations*, in 1989. He didn't even bother sending it out to publishers after watching Essex Hemphill successfully do the same. His dedication to publishing the works of gay Black writers was one of his biggest priorities. He focused on the visibility of gay Black poets, as these voices needed to be heard, especially those writers, who, without a platform, remained silenced. When we first met he already had a plan to publish one hundred gay Black poets in one collection. He had been told this feat could never be accomplished since one hundred gay Black poets didn't exist. He knew that was untrue and was now on a mission. In fact, there were so many submissions he had to turn poets away. He then immediately started planning a collection of two hundred gay Black poets for a future volume so he could include them. *The Road Before Us: 100 Gay Black Poets* was Assotto's baby. It brought him so much joy publishing this award-winning book. Winner of the Lambda Literary Award for Gay Men's Poetry in 1992, *The Road Before Us: 100 Gay Black Poets* led to smaller collections of poetry including *Here To Dare*, which featured ten gay Black poets, followed by *Milking Black Bull*, a collection of eleven gay Black poets which Assotto originally conceived for Galiens Press.

As his health deteriorated, Assotto was clear that his days were numbered, and through it all, he wrote. He created verse that would be read for many years to come. In his last poetry collection, *Wishing for Wings*, he took us along on his emotional journey. As Assotto focused on this collection, he knew he would be unable to get *Milking Black Bull* published, so we made arrangements with Vega Press to publish it instead. *Wishing For Wings* became the priority.

As the clock ticked and Assotto's emotions raged, he stayed focused on *Wishing For Wings*, which we tried so hard to publish before he passed. Unfortunately, we didn't manage it until two months after his death. It was Assotto's poetry collection *Stations* that signaled the beginning of Galiens Press and it was appropriate that his poetry, too, mark its end.

While writing *Wishing For Wings*, Assotto also had in mind a volume of his collected works that would be published posthumously as *Spells Of A Voodoo Doll*. This volume would include poetry, lyrics, essays, and performance texts. He was aware that his words should be presented in different forms, even if sometimes duplicated within the book. He found it important to present those words in every medium possible. That had always been his plan. He believed the human struggle for liberation would always be, so what better places to mirror this movement than on stage, in song, in books, or even through dance, sculptures, or paintings. It was not about being subtle. He was upfront, no hidden messages. He wanted to enlighten and teach everyone about difference, about respect, about freedom, and about growth. If an avenue did not present itself to do so, he created one.

As Assotto was writing and orchestrating the remaining years of his life, he also cared selflessly for and mentored many Black gay and lesbian writers. Their bonds were tight. They were people of beauty with words that stung. It was a wonderful time and a horrible time.

As Assotto's friends passed one by one, he was prepared, but not prepared for Jan's death. Not

feeling well himself, he still created a beautiful tribute to Jan's life: a plot in the Evergreens Cemetery,
where they lay together, with a headstone that reads
"Nuclear Lovers" beneath a photo of them both.
With his mom and some friends, we brought a quilt
panel Assotto made for Jan down to the 1993 March
on Washington to be included in the AIDS Memorial
Quilt. I arranged an evening of poetry that weekend
at the historic Evans-Tibbs home, where some of his
contributors and poet friends engaged in a powerful
evening of poetry. Assotto, although not feeling very
well at all, lay on the floor in the dining room and
mustered his way thru it.

In the months to come, he took time to plan for
his own death. Assotto had introduced me to his
mother Marie, who I called Mom. I watched him
and his mother butt heads, but I also witnessed an
extraordinary love between them. One day, Assotto
asked me to sit with him and his mother. He
wanted to talk about his death, his wishes. Sitting
in a large, throne-like chair, while his mother and
I sat in smaller chairs before him, Assotto discussed his imminent death. He gently explained
that he wanted me to handle his funeral arrangements. His mother said she was comfortable with
me fulfilling his wishes. He explained how he
wanted his coffin carried down Seventh Avenue,
with ACT UP members blocking the streets; laid
out who would speak and sing at his funeral. Every
single detail. His mother sat quietly and agreed to
it all. It was excruciating.

The night Assotto died, his mom and some
friends were at his apartment. We watched as
his mom frantically combed his hair and doused
him with cologne until the funeral director came
to remove his body. Everyone left the room, except

me. I watched as they placed his lifeless body in a black body bag. How could this fierce, outspoken, beautiful man be carried out of his home in this way? His presence was just zipped up forever. It is a memory I wish I never had.

Because time was of the essence, Assotto lived a lifetime in thirty-six short years. He lived lifetimes within a lifetime. I consider myself lucky to have shared that same lifetime as him. His ankh still hangs over the front door to my home. Twenty-nine years later, it is a reminder of Assotto's life. A reminder of life itself. As I wrote in the foreword of *Wishing For Wings*, "Well, my brother, you will always be in my heart and soul. You left me the responsibility to continue to bring your words to the world. Your voice may be silenced, but your legacy will forever live on."

Thank you for being interested in Assotto Saint's work. We will call his name forever. His legacy will remain always and forever in his words and activism. As Assotto said, "Dare To Be You! Dare To Be More!"

Sacred
Spells

In loving memory of my life-partner Jan Urban Holmgren

(April 25, 1939 – March 29, 1993)

As a poet and playwright, whose themes are mainly inspired by the gay black community, I am often told that I will always have a "limited" readership and audience. This implies that my writings perhaps will never enjoy broad commercial success. As though such success should be the primary gauge of an artist's works. Although I do want my writings to be published, staged, bought, read, discussed, and remembered, the perennial question that challenges me is not will my audience always be limited, but rather am I limiting myself?

When I started to write thirteen years ago, I felt a need to present the gay black experience, as I, an "openly" gay black man, lived it. And as others, meaning a non-gay and non-black readership and audience, seldom had the chance to acquaint themselves with it, except for the writings of Richard Bruce Nugent, Langston Hughes, and Samuel Delany. Their works always left me in a high spirit, deepening my appreciation of the past, but needing much more, especially in the field of nonfiction.

Right from the start, my writings, especially my plays (*Risin' to the Love We Need, Black Fag*, and *New Love Song*), became what I call a necessary theater. I was cognizant of the wants and needs of our emerging community; my writings needed to serve its visibility and empowerment. Most revolutions—be they political, social, spiritual, or economic—are usually complemented by one in literature. The Civil Rights Movement counted on numerous literary voices, from Maya Angelou to Bobby Seale, to fuel outrage and inspire justice, while Simone de Beauvoir, Betty Friedan, and Gloria Steinem led the feminist cause.

Along with a few other writers, most notably the members of the Blackheart Collective (whose founder, Isaac Jackson, was a ground-breaker in openly gay black publishing by putting out four issues of *The Blackheart Collective Journal*), and the late Philip Blackwell (writer of numerous plays, such as *Two Heads, A Lover's Play, City Men*, which was successfully produced), I not only committed myself toward an affirmation of the gay black community, but also toward the liberation of an audience from its own misconceptions of gay black life.

Occasionally I have been asked if I seriously expect non-gay blacks to identify with my writings. This infuriates me. It reminds me of the degree of my dehumanization, the extent of my oppression, and ultimately my invalidation as a gay black man.

Why should I not hope that any audience could identify with all these abstract yet very tangible things, which characterize my humanity. After all, I have had to identify with countless non-gay black characters. My pursuit of happiness is not unlike that of most human beings who, enthralled by the sensation of being alive, hunger for financial stability, thirst for spiritual fulfillment, and crave for love and respect through "family" and community.

As gay black poets and playwrights, we are persons of the roads still looking for the other side of the rainbow. The best answer to the question of who we are resides in our experiences; from whence our strongest writings are derived. Old myths explode as new ones of our own molding take their place, in turn recreating us.

While we map out this new wilderness of our

experiences, we must also bear witness. Like archaeologists, we have to file those reports in the form of our finely crafted poems and plays, which we must then make available to the world. It is our duty to share the writings with others, not just file them away in our computers or in our desk drawers. Our writings should very much be a public process that reflects private passions.

Yes, this telling of us will bring the pain of rejection. Too often, as gay black men, our lives have been so painful that we do not last beyond the pain. We can take all sorts of mental pills for the hurt, but painful feelings are destroyed once we start to pinpoint them, analyze them, and write about them. Dodging these emotions or being frightened by them gets us nowhere. Any learning process involves fear. We overcome fear when it ceases to hamper our ability to tell the truth, something writers have to vigilantly, even violently, guard.

We must fight our numerous detractors, who will try to block our visions as well as the world's visions of us. Nor can we cover our own eyes from the glaring sunlight and pretend that it is night.

When we sacrifice our authenticity as gay black writers "to pass" in order to secure a book contract from a major publishing house (nowadays, most of the large companies are actively seeking out gay authors), when we sell out our dreams, thereby causing our art to mask our true feelings, when we inhabit a world of lies, which turn us into frauds in our own language and ideas, we resign ourselves to the status quo of this unsettling world we live in.

We must become whistle-blowers. We must become muthafuckhas with messages and a mission. We must become powerful enough to stand tall and not fall, thrive and not just survive. A tremendous amount of common sense, arrogance, and defiance will get us through.

America is a capitalist society. Let us save, beg, and borrow money to keep building our autonomous publications and other cultural institutions. Let us make sure that these institutions outlast us and do not become self-serving. Let us live beyond the here and now by nurturing each other and supporting one another's works.

Although we should not let the "white" gay and the "straight" black literary publications and theater institutions off the hook for tokenizing, not publishing our writings, or not producing our plays, we cannot make grievances the primary focus of our writings or of our lives. So much of gay and black art depicts its heroes as victims, in a realm of reverie or on the roads to calvary, constantly at the mercy of others. Puzzling over our predicaments and commitments, we can be skeptical, but never comfortable in the cynical blame game.

Nor can we take the high road behind our writings and evade our social responsibility as human beings to dirty our hands and feet when we need to publicly pick and kick shit out of our way. This especially applies to the handful of us who have proudly and productively assumed either the "gay black writer" or "black gay writer" label and benefited from our tokenization and overpresentation. The promise of a new world order lives not just in our words, but in our actions.

We should not just try to internalize our oppression through our writings, but externalize it by fighting bigotry tooth and nail, no matter what form it takes. Whether it's in confronting AIDS, apartheid, dictatorships, homophobia, racism, sexism, anti-Semitism, and silence that's foisted upon us or that we force upon ourselves. Our destiny must always be confronted with our conscience.

In this current health crisis, many of us gay black writers are dying much sooner than we anticipated. The numbers are already overwhelming. Thirteen contributors to the anthology *The Road Before Us: 100 Gay Black Poets*, which I edited and published in November 1991, have so far died. Among these dead are such notables as Melvin Dixon, David Frechette, Roy Gonsalves, Craig G. Harris, and Donald Woods. Over half of the contributors to the same volume are people with AIDS (PWAs), such as myself, or have tested HIV-positive. The same ratio applies to previous gay black anthologies such as *In the Life* (Alyson Publications, 1986), edited by Joseph Beam, who died of AIDS in 1988, and *Brother to Brother* (Alyson Publications, 1991), edited by Essex Hemphill, who is open about his seropositive status. Five of the fifteen editors of the first volume of *Other Countries: Black Gay Voices*, which was published in 1988, have since died of AIDS. *Sojourner: Black Gay Voices in the Age of AIDS*, recently published by the Other Countries collective, lists in the bio section almost one half of its contributors as dead or living with/dying of AIDS. Its chief editor, B. Michael Hunter, is seropositive, as is Rodney Dildy, the editor and publisher of *The Pyramid Periodical*, one of our three gay black literary journals. The HIV's death toll in our community keeps beating its drum with no abatement in sight.

We must strive before it is too late to realize this creative wish: that the writings of our experiences serve as testaments to those who passed along this way, testimonies to our times, and legacies to future generations. These works should offer our readers and audience inspiration, consolation, and hope in the advent of a new millennium. Our words indeed do triumph over silence, despair, and death.

As our strength is constantly being tested, the only time to play it safe is inside our coffins. Even then, when we are disfigured by the horrors of HIV, we should morally and legally leave instructions for our life-partners, families, and friends not to close the damn caskets, not to hide or deny the real cause of our deaths, not to falsely rewrite our history in our obituaries. So what if people are uncomfortable!

I don't ever want to show anyone my physical and psychological wounds and scars without telling them what caused me to hurt, what it will take to heal me, and what collectively and responsibly should be done to prevent similar injuries from ever happening again—to me or to others.

In these dire times, I'd much rather engage myself reading works that are didactic and political instead of precious and arty stuff, where there's a lack of passion, integrity of feelings, sense of commitment beyond the self; but this constant romanticization of inertia, unfulfilling sex, along with the usual indulgence in alcohol and substance abuse because mother/father were not loving enough. Tired shit!

To the original question: Am I limiting myself? I answer emphatically, "No." Through poetry and playwriting I go to the limits of my being to forever discover the essence of rebirth within. I explore the world and how it closes in on itself with its prejudices. My poems and plays are weapons and blessings that I use to liberate myself, to validate our realities as gay black men, and to elucidate the human struggle. What better place to celebrate this movement than on the page and on the stage.

Lately I have been accused of not practicing the gospel I preach of "truth at all costs." That by using the pen name Assotto Saint, instead of my birth-given name, Yves F. Lubin, I am protecting my family from being shamed by my outrageousness and by my openly gay black writings. This invites a three-fold answer that I hope will clarify matters.

I have never denied, lied, or invoked "the right of privacy" regarding my two names. When I was born out of wedlock in Haiti in 1957, my mother—rightfully so in her hurt and anger—refused to give me my father's name, which is Mercier. She passed to me her own family's name of Lubin. I chose the pseudonym Assotto Saint when I started writing in 1980 to recreate myself amidst all this mess. By 1972, I had already come out to every member of my family, our friends, and the New York Haitian community and media.

Assotto is the Creole pronunciation of a fasci-nating-sounding drum in the voodoo religion. At one point I had taken to spelling Assotto with one "t" but superstitiously added back the other "t" when my CD4 t-cell count dropped down to nine. Saint is derived from Toussaint L'Ouverture, one of my heroes. By using the *nom de guerre* of Saint, I also wanted to add a sacrilegious twist to my life by grandly sanctifyin the loud low-life bitch that I am.

"Bilolo!
Ayida pas nan betise oh.
Ayida pas nan betise ave yo.
Enle, langaille oh.
Ayida pas nan betise oh
Ayida pas nan betise ave yo.
Ca qui vle content content.
Ca qui vle fache fache oh.
Ayida oh
Ayida pas nan bestise ave you."

"Ayida Pas Nan Betise"
(Petro Dance)

"Sanba sa fe mal o
Ma rele sanba ma rele
Sanba fa mal o
Gade sa ne g-yo fe mwen
Sanba san-m ap koule
You ban m cyay-la pote
M pa sa pote!
Chay-la lou wo ma roule
Chay-la lou wo m pa sa pote!
Ma roule!"

"Ke-M Pa Sote"
Boukman Eksperyans

Poems

Selections from *Triple Trouble*

[Tongues Untied]

Soul

I remember the beginning
a dream ancient as dawn
a dream of destiny drumming up
the blood
the flesh
this earth
a dream we were once one
soul

Ghosts

both posed
in the backroom's shadows
caught
in memories of promises
kisses
some sunrise long ago
yet
neither said hello

I Want to Celebrate

i want to celebrate vicious-officious cocks
that kind with a hook or mushroom head
cast spells
made me lose consciousness when most alive
forced to acquiesce to grace under pressure
holiness in being truly low

i want to celebrate cushiony groins
hot balls that were a mouthful
tough titties with clip marks
hairy fists armed with magic twists
& this well-greased ass
that took pleasure in its added dimensions

i want to celebrate all those tops cowboys & cops
all those last calls when
a stranger's smile posed no danger
then in my instinct i trusted
a past i ransack
now my hands are my best friends

Sacrifice

we wanted wine
the simple charm of a bottle
the toasts
the bouquet
a melody for memory
a memory for melody
our fears never faded with a kiss
there's madness this moment
the bottle falls
in a ritual of threats
sharp shards cut
we are suckers for each other's
spilled blood

Widower

for jim

his is the pain that bloats
then suffocates
memories crush thoughts into choked up words
silent screams pant for wind
every step heaves heavy
time tolls
one
his is the pain which cannot stop
till he falls
too

The Geography of Poetry

for ntozake shange

ntozake shange
i looked you up
among the poets at barnes & noble
but i didn't find you

walt was there amidst leaves of grass
anne gazed down
her glazed eyes dreamt of rowing mercy
erica posed in her latest erotica
even rod took much space
i searched among ghosts
& those alive
still
i couldn't find you

i asked the clerk
if he had kept you tied down in boxes
or does he use your books as dart boards
he smirked then shouted "she's in the black section
in the back"
even literature has its ghettos

stacked amongst langston, nikki, & countee
maya who looked mad
the blues had her bad
zake tell me
did you demand to be segregated
"does color modify poetry"
i asked the manager

he patted me on my head
whispered
"it's always been this way"

Shores

i remember
makkis sailing the aegean sea
on breakfast of feta baklava & sunshine
pepe rafting through floating gardens
while on a siesta of mariachi y margaritas
abdullah who sliced the golden nile with his felucca
bits of pita beans & english falling from his lips
olive-skinned mario of the gondolas who enchanted me
with pasta pasolini & stars then arrivederci
they all chattered about anchoring their dreams
on america's shores
but do they know that our lady in the harbor
milks
us
immigrants
of
the
honey
in
our
blood

Epitaph

there's a grave in your heart
father holed
where over & over you lay
to bury yourself
through thirty years of fits furies & fangs
ground zero

***

here lives she
whose womb is a wound

Triple Trouble

An Exorcism

"Cops Lock Up Gay Sex Den"
"Long Island Grandma Dead of AIDS"
"Bachelors Forcing Sex Ed on Kids"
—headlines, *The New York Post*

Last July 4th, like every July 4th for four years,
Nile ground ginger roots and lime rind, spooned
brown sugar in a cup of Cockspur rum he gulped.

Carrying on his head
all the front pages
        of the New York Post for the past year
all the front pages
        with sorry stories
all the front pages
        with mad headlines
which had struck and hurt his eyes,
he climbed the stairs of his abandoned
building on Eighth Street between B & C.

In the center of the cement rooftop,
he heaped the papers
on which he gracefully stripped.
He rubbed greek-imported olive oil
over his body to catch more heat.

Staring straight at the sun
        Nile waited to feel the voice
staring straight at the sun
        Nile waited to feel the beat

staring straight at the sun
        Nile waited till his teeth clacked
with a shriek so hot it set the heap on fire.

Round and round the flames he ran,
talking in tongues.

Then, on the roof's edge,
he perched in arabesque
like an eagle ready for flight.
High above his head, he lifted his arms.
In his fluttering fingers, the sun shattered.
The universe stood still while Nile smiled.
An empowering mystery,
the past passed on from generations,
all the joy of life reflected.

So slowly his body bent forward.
Long supple arms opened low
to pay homage
to surrender himself in prayer
to offer himself

        a black queen   dancing with shadows
               at high noon.

triple trouble that's brutal
chasing America's evil spirits away.

Stations

. . . .

"This is the long-distance call"

—Paul Simon

Processional

in the name of america
beyond masks labels beacon
you with viking tales
sired in the snows of sundsvall
i brick-dark
from the country of loas coconuts toussaint
keys chains hankies hang out of your pockets
pearls from my ear
trusting togetherness
your voice of fugues
my pen which paints heaven in hell
on this land of unsettled promises
bearing eros christ oya as talismans
we caravan

Rite of Passage

```
tripping
h
r
o          a
u          c o k e
g          i
high speed
      l
   clock
      w
```

i. never trick with a friend

```
      v
s c a l e s
      n        e
   bull older
      s    f  g
              e
          m
          a
          d
          n
       poet
          s
          s
```

ii. never trick with someone you work with

```
c l o u d s
   f

 a m  b l a c k
   e
   m         h
 s o  w h i t e
    r       s
    y
            f
            l
            y
            i
            n
            g
```

iii. never trick with someone who lives in our building

```
                          o  p
                         t
 r e s t l e s s  o n  r o o f

l o o k
      d
      o
      w
      n
          c a t c h  t h e  b i g  a p p l e
                      m
                      p
                      i
                      r
              s t a t e  o f  d e s i r e
        g       t
        a m e r i c a
        s       l
        p       l
```

iv. never trick in our apartment except for a threesome

```
         o
         u
         f r e e d o m
                 a
         h       m
         t e c h n o l o g y
         a       s
         r
         t


  s i n c e   a l l   t h a t   w e  a r e
                     h
                     i
         h o u r ' s
         o             e
         l             c
         d                 o
         s                     n
                             d
```

v. never trick more than once with the same guy

```
s h i b b o l e t h
         o
         o
         m
         e
l o v e r
  v       a
  e       n
  r e a g a n  e l e c t i o n
             o
             v
             e
             m
             b
             e
         r a i n b o w
```

36

vi. never trick with an ex-lover

t
h e e d t h e a u t o
e   m
r   a
e   t
                            i
                   v o i c e

vii. never fail to tell a trick that you do have a lover

  p r e g n a n t
  r
  o
  m
  i n
d e m o c r a c y
            n
            y
            o
            n
     d r e a m s

viii. never exchange home or business phone numbers
       with a trick

```
we will
   r
 sing
  t  a
  e  l
    new
       n
  gospel
```

*ix. **never lie if one asks about the other's tricks***

```
come out of it
           i
           n
      ahead of time


           home
           u
           r


           w
           a
    close eyes
    r
    a
    d
    l
  the


      d
        e
          c
         a
          l
            o
           g
            u
             e
```

*x. **never forget that our love is not a trick***

Lord Have Mercy

manacled on a cross of purple
leather pillows puffed with lamentations
buffed by the sweat of strapped angels
straddled through infernal nights of rites
savage souls salvaged
in the flicker of a votive candles-circle
i watched baldhead gabriel genuflect
frail naked freckled like a leopard
the morning after
he had worn his whiteness best in black
armored crusader in rhythm
"i don't remember
your name" his cruel lips curled
"it doesn't matter i have
a lover" i sighed unmasked
in blessed remission
like a priest he kissed
then uncuffed my feet

Overnight in Mykonos

so the beat for the bacchanal
was born between moonbeams
on this island
of schemes dreams screams
drunk on elixir
of midnight madness' rhymes
come on satyr
shake your laughter
at the stars
sing with me
"so many men so little time"

Glory

to display grace flesh lust
under wondrous spells
of that aztec goddess of the crops
worshiped atop the moon pyramid
on our first pilgrimage
across the border
this hour's elemental ritual
roar of rapturous rebirth
you are scorched earth
i breeze dewdrops

In the Fast Lane

riding
we kept riding
on los angeles' freeways
up down the baths' roller coaster
that afternoon of smog summer sand
through a night of fog lure sweat
at the wheels of a rented red honda
at the wheels of desire
you hummed along airwaves
conscious in continuous flight
i weaved
shuffling nonstop
memories
a thought
moods
a voice
metaphors
an image
bulletin blares
our unconscious captured
with prophetic fanfare
in momentary lapse
some strange gay plague
not a word echoed
i looked at you look at me
not a word echoed
some strange gay plague
in momentary lapse
with prophetic fanfare
our unconscious captured

bulletin blares
an image
metaphors
a voice
moods
a thought
memories
shuffling nonstop
i weaved
conscious in continuous flight
you hummed along airwaves
at the wheels of desire
at the wheels of a rented red honda
through a night of fog lure sweat
that afternoon of smog summer sand
up down the baths' roller coaster
on los angeles' freeways
we kept riding
riding

Souvenir

tracing back dirt roads
i wanted to write a happy carefree poem
for my country

turquoise skies
amethyst mountains
emerald oceans
acres upon acres of sugar cane
miles upon miles of rice fields
thousands upon thousands of coconut trees
all shimmering in the seas' breeze
drumbeats that strike thunderclaps
pipe-puffing ladies in colorful dresses
candle-stiff under baskets
of guavas mangos papayas
ripe with sweetness

i wanted to write a happy carefree poem
for my childhood
lost too fast thirteen years ago
somewhere in the air
between port-au-prince & new york city
but i'm left bereft
by faces with no traces of smiles
eyes without vision

in postcards
haiti is the pearl of the islands
hallmark trick
in 1983

haiti is a cemetery
streets packed with zombies
souls sold to baby doc
who boogies in palais national
like baron samedi
even the banda lost its rhythm

skinny carrefour hustlers
tickle their dicks
for those few tourists
who still dare
ensnared by magic

every other woman's belly is laden
with another baby
every other man's head is laden
with another figurine to sculpt
canvas to paint
tap-tap to drive

"bon dié bon oui" preaches the priest
who carries a camera
records confessions
for loups-garous tontons macoute
the land is parched
with ash of infected swine
everywhere hands stretch out of time
to anyone
for anything

South African Roadblocks

through barbed wire
beyond squatters' camp

in need of the sky
two black boys reach
forbidden horizons

bullets bark
sniff blood botha

Howard Beach

1.
epithets bats tire iron shatter
the late night
a black man beseeches his god
not to let him fall on calvary
mercury flashes pluto summons
away from America
may he discover her

2.
i shake off the nightmare's sweat
to cleanses my soul
i shake it off to cleanse history
cold sweat this water is no blessing
the rage in me climbs out
to free the sun
in our sky of clouds

Offertory on a Seventh Anniversary

on this day
when there's no holiness
in all this madness
of tests turncoats threats
where the heart is
with the sharpest brass knife
let us carve a tiny star
on each other's chest
watch them light up
bright red
we will bless them with our lips
drink life
neither a seven-year itch
nor death
can split

The Memory of Suffering

anonymous
high-risk statistics
past my cowardice accusations
through your lingering cold
months after i had stepped by myself
same office without windows
late-posted warnings
coded files
cheerful counselor
who knew all the answers
she told me then
tells you now
what was suspected
all along
we clutched each other
too numb to cry

ARC-EN-CIEL

a)
it may all be a related complex
the guessing game bargained
relentless rehearsal of a danse macabre
self-portrait foreshadowed
innocence hums a carol
demons laugh

> *did he ever tell you*
> *he believed in his immaculate conception*
> *till he was thirteen*
> *he's lived bastardly since*
> *each moment a sacrilege*

b)
infectious questions trigger deficient
quicksand fills his chelsea flat
he opens the window
even the void looks too empty to fit in
now he doesn't see it
catholic guilt syndrome

> *did he ever tell you*
> *despite his mother's denial*
> *he was a wednesday's child*
> *some witch prophesied*
> *wouldn't live past thirty*

c)
low immunity amidst swollen pits
a crucifix guidepost hangs bare
he reaches through decades
to trace birth-acquired marks
to transmute nightmare screams daily into blessings
to pray that the healer messiah in him is born

Pater Noster

father my father
laius liar liable
doomed by the oracle of blood
where the soul burns
never a daily bread sacrifice
fuel of lowest temptations
ash of forgiveness smiles revelations
still too hot
father my father
laius liar liable
damned be thy name

Mater Dolorosa

night
after night
a mother bends over
her son's bones sores scales
writhing on his bed
fit for a king
satin sheets sweat secrets
she closes
his blurry eyes
rolls rosary beads
faithful
in the morning
he'll wake up
to see her
smile

This Hour's Death

for joe caballero

2:03 a.m.
two lovers
one in sleep twists
the other bored with the late movie
both shaken by insistent rings
one picks up hesitant then screams
guessing the other runs to the bedroom

2:24 a.m.
cautious steps greeted by a scavenger
in mask gown sanctity
she drags a screeching stretcher
the friend lays wrapped up
"lazarus rise" one wishes
doubtful the other checks the pulse
deafening in its silence

2:31 a.m.
torn
one speaks to him
the other of him
across deserted corners
one chokes on tears
the other shoulders a red plastic bag

3:00 a.m.
candles glow ghost petals shadows
in a bowl of holy water
rippled by pleas
to soothe another restless night passage

one prays hums chants
the other sips coffee
ponders who will be next

De Profundis

for eleven gay men in my building

his shades of blossoms ties
that thread-thin silver bells bracelet
always laced round his left wrist
late-night strolls through chelsea
with mini carmen aida his poodles
the summer-long peach tans
come-on-boy-let's-dance glance at the cockring
torrid tales of travels
strangers of all colors nested never long
studio of strobes walled by books opera disco
he craved french fries kiwis gin
i tried to see anything but his casket
gorged by the ground
the tears were for myself
one day
i shall be in this
darkness

Rest in Peace

for lew voyles

i woke up by the laughter
of girls skipping rope
loop lollipops boy-talk
memories lit back years of saturday nights
at flamingo saint moonshadow
menergized you dervished
with your dimples drugs giggles
suddenly from my vision your face sprang
hung like the holy shroud
even through death
you are crossing states

Hosanna

for reverend charles angel, jr

birds of a feather coo
spread their wings
at the edge of the world
they soar
stretching themselves
to god

Heaven in Hell

for counsel wright

there stood a blue-eyed booted brute
chaps cap smile of steel
the kind we knelt to in backrooms
on your third anniversary
in remembrance i slaved
headful of poppers
mouthful of cum
soulful of heaven
may i never know
that hellfire of fevers
with which your breath burned
out

Relics

*"How strange that I'm alive. A bland,
efficient death searches this age . . ."*
—Miklós Radnóti

i.
mama gunda never said there'd be
nights like these
she never told you of the heart
with its pitfalls
does she hate me
i rushed you back to america
favorite of five offspring
she blesses on your yearly pilgrimage
rebel who deserted her window's shrine
sweden's borders
to sail gaily around the world
like a sea gull
desolate new yorker
on a two-week escape
broken midway by multiple phone calls
confessions of not trusting myself
pleas turned threats

ii.
that night
the full moon looked mean
big enough to bite
on a hegira from bar to bar
tempted i teased
fearful

60

iii.
remember those megatron men
eyes of skies no tear clouded
bodies chiseled by our manly caresses
lips of air wine sweet talk
watch them lean on canes
a faithful's arm
hardly crossing streets
before cars rush
drop-dead beauties

iv.
walk me to the anvil
no acid smile lights up the darkness
touch that padlock on the mineshaft door
everard boarded
relics of a revolution
crusaded
not long enough

The Wedding

nesting against your chest
unsafe in all this sorrow
dim light shine upon us
o constitution
commandments for a new world's testament
tabernacle of the american dream
reached with our rainbows lambdas unicorns
rebels we vow never to bow
on these caving grounds
dare be more
man & man

The Quilt

this is not the fire island sand but molten lava
we are burning you talk strange land i stalk
cross-country fabric handsewn name panels sequins bulletins
daily road of photographs painted resistance flashes pennants
albums whistle jockstrapped cats tuxedo stars t-shirt butterflies
feather dolls leather bears patchworked lives cut three by short

joe / testimonies / counsel / memories / lew / fantasies /
it's them / they were here / it's them / they were here /

pinch myself no tv mixed media homo epidemic hemo quarantine
virus junkie the blood hiv test semen rockhudson kaposi's cdc
t-cells liberace pneumocystis bad blood terrydolan antibodies azt
voodoo arc a 1721 africa roycohn opportunistic gmhc condoms nih
always the blood michaelbennett willismith carriers gaetandugas
asshole president commission syphilis positive safe sex vaccine

joe / testimonies / counsel / memories / lew / fantasies /
it's them / they were here / it's them / they were here /

we might not make it through the fog grids display epitaphs full
circle headache grips art faint thunder the skies dark clouds
perhaps kleenex cry sap strength bereavement project burdens
horrific holocaust imagery in this tragedy 100% futile
judeo-christianity infamy in this travesty 100% fatal
our country 'tis of teflon gipper's bushshit

joe / testimonies / counsel / memories / lew / fantasies /
it's them / they were here / it's them / they were here /

The March

too young
let us not fall like cattle
to redeem america's
plaguing prejudices
let us not fall
let us

savagely charge a country
tempted by fascism
our martyrdom is no fake slaughter
but terror is a syndrome
which can act up
like bleeding black bulls

too young
let us not fall like cattle
to redeem america's
plaguing prejudices
let us not fall
let us

Chosen of Places

"To the Egyptians, the east bank of the Nile was the land of the living.
Here they built their villages, their palaces, and their grand temples.
As the capital of Egypt for the better part of 1,500 years, Thebes (now
Luxor) had plenty of time to develop into a glorious city. There are
no traces of its temporal glory—the mud-brick palaces of kings and
nobles—but its spiritual grandeur still survives in two of the temples:
*Karnak and Luxor."**

come with me
to karnak
house of amon-ra
king
of the gods
in the silence
of stones
only the dirt knows
the sacred
secrets

"The temple of Karnak is about two miles north of the center of town.
It's a bit of a hike for those who like to walk, and if you'd rather ride,
there are plenty of hantours around. You should be able to bargain
for a one-way ride of about LE 1 ($1.40), and a driver will wait for
you and bring you back for LE 2 ($2.80). It's a very pleasant walk in
*the evening, but be sure to wear sturdy shoes."**

open your eyes
scan
the crumbling pylon's
horizon

hail
forty sphinxes
that guard the gateway
to the myth
hundreds of queens
pharaohs
kings
enlarged
enhanced

encumbered
follow me
into this complex
dream
of giants'
consciousness

there are columns,
capitals,
colonnades
see statues,
colossi,
obelisks
there are carvings,
pillars,
a hypostyle hall
see shrines,
kiosks,
courts
where ramses
hatsepsut
set prayed
akhenaton scribed
heretic hymns

no tiny sanctuary
to amon,
mut,
khon's triad
this is a city
no intact liturgy
through kingdoms,
periods,
dynasties
this is a festival
no planned procession
between pylons,
porticoes,
pavilions
this is a carousel
round-round-round the scarab
whisper our wish
into the lake's
primeval waters
become one
to our demythologized
age
void
of salvation
close our eyes

*"Karnak Temple is open daily from about 7 a.m. until 5 p.m. Admission is LE 1 ($1.40). Every day but Friday, there's a Sound and Light Show in a variety of languages. The English version is presented on Monday, Wednesday, and Saturday, starting at 7:30 p.m. (The time often changes during Ramadan, so check to be sure if you come during that month). Tickets are LE 2 ($2.80)."**

come
to karnak
magical legacy
man's awareness immemorial
in these hieroglyphs
behold
the key of life

*"The west bank was, for the Pharaohs, the land of the dead. Every
evening, they saw the sun "die" behind the Theban hills, so they, too,
went to the west after death."**

* *Frommer's Dollarwise Guide to Egypt* by Nancy McGrath, published by Simon & Schuster,
New York, 1982–1983 Edition.

Arabian Horse

a lone
old man stood in the sunset
his galabieh large with wind
frowns of dirt crowned by a koufieh
chipped teeth yellow with years
the softest eyes

"american"   he asked   "welcome
tomorrow take you to other side
valley of the king's   valley of the queens
no   why   want sex
me big" he grabbed his hard-on "big like horse"

i smiled
kissed both his cheeks
strolled along
he laughed
cursed mad in arabic
neighed a strange tune to the moon

Nuclear Lovers

"And the 20th century is dead,
and the 21st century is dead,
and the 22nd century is dead,
and the 23rd century is full of fairies!"
—Carl Morse

soon

as they sound the alarm

let us run to the river

where we first met

sat many a sunset

there

with bare hands

we will dig a deep hole

in the earth

lay together

centuries later

when they excavate

they shall hear two hearts

regenerate love

in the universe

Wishing for Wings

"You took me to your heart, religious like an oath, I brought you my love divine, the hands of faith, the breath of hope, brush soft across my face, each day is like the kiss of an angel. I've found heaven here on earth, a dream come true with your love. The stars collide with every touch, my world is joy, devotion so immense so strong it hurts, I close my eyes and all I see is you, my prayers will all be answered, if you stay."

—Jimmy Somerville

Writing About AIDS

to akhenaton

when the pen dries
when the pencil breaks
when the computer crashes
swallow your spit & bite yourself hard
acts of despair can't be calmed by pretense of circumstance
at the mercy of an age where horrific images hang
in an oblivious silence that draws poetry
which must be written
with blood

Life-Partners

between
solitudes of illness
& beatitudes our lips utter
evening settles in this exile of senses for our surrender
one more friend's death has clocked the day like a tolling bell
biding time we are shadows also shrinking early into destiny
let us gather our pills & swallow all regrets with a kiss
cover each other then weave
dreams of another day
to come

On the Pulse of Night

startled out of sleep i look around
the room swamped in a nightmare of silence
not even the faintest snore to let me know you are still alive

fearing hushed calls gone unheard
my heart breaks in the wake of spirits that quake the ground
my tongue curls dry with a cry

i don't call your name & there's no sound as my hand slides
across these bed sheets to hold your wrist
feel your pulse race through me

Shuffle Along

hooked up
to the same pole
i.v. garlands
of cytovene & pentamidine
unravel queer patterns
of a survival ritual
that strings us
thread-thin yet tight
as life-partners
trapped in this marathon
of disintegration

the rhythm mutates
like the noxious virus
inside collapsing veins
& atrophied muscles
blurry eyes swirl
round the dying room
dizzily we drag on
carry each other
through the 11th hour
clinging desperately
while time ticks

Lady & Me

1.

quarter past eight
every weekday mo`rning
white fake-leather bag
strapped on fat laps
she settles the same corner
at rico's in midtown where
puertoriquenos y dominicanos
thunder greetings with orders
in a lightning of spanish
discuss el diario's headlines
gobble the $1.99 special
of huevos con cuchifritos
bet numbers with pepe
the bookie waiter who
jokes around & laughs while
some of us curse & wait
for honey-glazed donuts
hot-toasted buttered bagels
& the best cafe con leche
this side of the atlantic

2.

hazel eyes look out past
a multitude of robots
mannequins marching
in the garment district
delicate seamstress fingers
lift an already full cup
into which she slowly stirs
many packets of sugar
she licks the spoon dry
the steam always halos
her freckled caramel face
like i caught her today
back from my sick leave
thirty pounds skinnier
out of breath & uneasy
about returning to work
i sat down next to her
with a large frosty *bandito*
she gazed at the ghost of me
asked *"amigo, como esta"*

Don't Ask, Don't Tell, Don't Pursue

straddle
a stranger's head
slide your dick
'tween licking lips

his throat takes it
sweet & deep
pump his face
ride on

you tense up
he bites down
to prevent you
from pulling out

c'mon
unclamp his teeth
shut your eyes
shoot

standing
he whispers
"why didn't you
give me the load"

eyebrows raised
button your 501s
pat his back
hurry home

fingers
crusted with cum
fill in the day's
diary entry

"to understand
the phenomenon
of whales
beaching themselves

step inside
a backroom bar
discover
a colony of men

on their knees
or bent over
in an open chorus
of viral wails"

Contagion

for michael evans, m.d.

bricks
knots
shards in chest

robot
rushing out
of another hospital's
packed elevator

to bring a friend
bouquets again

greeted
once more by
a skeletal warrior's
respirator hiss

you
too
barely breathe

Rerun

for vito russo

chin up, tee-shirt
fast feet cross ninth avenue
blueness of skies
on the most beautiful day
when spring unwraps sweet & soft
like the cone you lick
with the sun in your smile
the sun everywhere, all over
even under mustache hair
mouth wide open
your eyes swallow whole
this corner of chelsea
in your throat: sun
then suddenly you choke
memory regurgitates
last year/vito loped/right here
freeze-frame
vision burns
ice cream drips

Audre's Apples

for audre lorde

as i swallow
the last morsel of a little green apple
blessed with myrrhed prayers & libations on an african altar

in a gothic cathedral
where with banners from all corners of our country
freed from the prejudice of a dozen years' politics of greed

thousands gather on king's day
to ground sorrow at a sister's recent passing
(lorde we testify)
drum up her spirit along a cascading rainbow
to the orishas' paradise

the juice snakes sweetly down my throat & circles my veins
it loosens my tingling toes stiffened
by neuropathy

armed only with a white candle that flares its last flames
i march out into the dark hell of
our big apple

False Starts

racing away
from campaign promises back to bushshit policies
watch him jiggle his fat ass while he jogs/
a man with obviously no big-stick dick
slick willie starts to make me sick/

what's the deal bill
bending over so fast on gays in the military
to nunn the hun who needs a laxative
& thinks that he not you should be in the white house/
stop playing political expediency games with civil rights/

what's the deal bill
with those HIV positive haitians
granted political asylum but isolated
in guantanamo's roach & rat-infested tents
under mean eyes of armed & gloved soldiers/

what's the deal bill
with appointing as an aids czar
a straight white woman from oregon
a least likely candidate to acquire the disease/
is that hillary's idea of sisterhood overhauling health care/

tell me mr. president
should i already write you off as the front runner
who would dash over hurdles to blaze us into a new millennium/
several of us are keeping tabs on your false starts/

The Mourning Song

to walter holland

night of memory mired in metaphors
virus-spittle rituals cough up tongue-tied elegies
the funk of fever lingers on lips that kissed dying eyes

contagion besieges the city
this house hallucinates corpses babbling behind walls
diva in despair, you howl arias of wrath no one but your heart hears

blind with sorrow, stumble out of bed to splash water over your head
pull up the window shades—then arms folded around your chest
let the dawn draw you into its promise

such silence mourns desire, are you worthy of this sunrise
through the frailty of fog, bursts of light echo
witness, you are graced to bear

Wishing for Wings

3 a.m., in the farthest corner, anxiety fogs the eyes
above a skyline of city lights, signs, & satellites

slow drift. . .acceptance finally of all that is inevitable,
when the human dwarfs by circumstance, (then a virus?)

yet the heart, how it expands in godless collapse,
breath floats feverish-high while you hear nothing

but "ah". . . bouncing back from the plate glass window,
shadows of a patient with his partner lean, (o life!)

side by side, in this hallway overlooking east where
the sun soon shall rise. form, figures, & faith blur

Vital Signs

for david frechette

medical absurdities multiply in necessity
stripping all dignity
low rate

there is this masked ball
nurses waltz out their delirium of blood
cold black hands; this hour, friends are few
how could six months elapse without a vanity mirror
our brother, our brother: how it was
to be alive

unearth
from a pillow of sorrow
the logic of illusions—just that, only that—
wrapped with fungi, your tongue sprouts no more metaphors
but the will endures like eucalyptus
oasis of fear

every minute or so
your red traffic-light eyes glare
& ward off the ghost who like a crow
looms to swallow your guts
numb your body into
a corpse

The Perfect Moment

rush of cusswords after the specialists stutter their apologetic bullshit
his belabored body bloated like some fowl fattened for slaughter
he smiles as you rest your head on his cathetered chest

that he remembers this man-to-man ritual you are grateful
in the coldness of a hospital room time typifies itself
moment of truth when winged dreams skid on a caged prayer

hands cupped against your cheeks he lifts your chin up
bright-eyed as numerous times before but now stare at death
lumps wedged in throat pledge eternal love & never mean it more

A Lover's Diary

monday, march 29, 1993

-01-
vigil on two chairs
i whisper "hey, good morning"
he doesn't respond
i watch his labored breathings
the headnurse suctions him up

02-
"he's turned for the worse"
doctor mcmeeking mumbles
weeks, days, just can't tell
"hours" insists my mother
furious i escort her out

-

-03-
the oscars come on
the crying game stars don't win
hoping he can hear
i remind him he's my light
death rattles my scream for help

-04-
the nurse rushes in
mother returns with prayers
i cradle him close
pleading "stay, one more day, stay"
eleven twenty, he's gone

-05-
bathe him with my tears
parched lips thirst for a wet kiss
i stick my tongue deep
bitter taste of bloody phlegm
moans spat out i shut his eyes

tuesday, march 30, 1993

-06-

cool one a.m. mist
edge of christopher street piers
alone with questions
high-tide waves whistle my name
in reflection, i stand still

-07-

call his three brothers
cold-heart swedes, they seldom
called
our closest friends gasp
call american airlines
his supervisor's voice cracks

-08-

find that damn letter
life insurance company
as of april first
slashing benefits by half
ha, he died march twenty-ninth

-09-

"this casket" i tell
the funeral director
chuckling "best we got
a mahogany beauty
five grand"—mace says "go for it"

-10-

tears & sympathy
people ask what they can do
well-meaning cliches
under such circumstances
coping as best as i can

wednesday, march 31, 1993

-11-
oatmeal, toast & juice
once again i fix too much
sorrow sucks my breath
bits of spoonfuls i can't eat
nauseous, i rush to the sink

-12-
mail-room announcement
posted with a cute picture
jan u. holmgren died
memorial viewing hours
shrewd neighbors saw this coming

-13-
i pick out the plot
down a hill, it faces west
there's a bench nearby
akhenaton & i sit
the salesman shrugs his consent

-14-
"sweetheart, see you soon"
will read the ribbon that wraps
the spray i order
fifty-three new-red roses
one for each year of his life

-15-
"two thousand fifty"
an operator tells me
the death notice costs
all the news that's fit to print
don't come cheap in this city

thursday, april 1, 1993

-16-
wake up, sleepy head
this ain't no april fool joke
you're on overload
cool down with a long shower
your head's about to explode

-17-
last-minute tie-up
full flight, airline breaks promise
"two passes, that's it"
stranded in Stockholm, only
one brother travels with his wife

-18-
account funds transferred
the bank manager calms down
brochures stacked in hand
she asks "what you plan to do
with that insurance money"

-19-
silk italian suit
flashy tie & keyboard scarf
shirt, shorts, belt, socks, shoes
the mortician gets them all
he swears he'll fix him up fine

-20-
printed the program
pedro did a superb job
jan would have been proud
read it over & over
then swallow three tylenols

friday, april 2, 1993

-21-
blur of a headache
like some mad zombie i zoom
through lateness & sweat
wrapped in grand african garb
open up, streets, ground me in

-22-
climb the parlor's stairs
request a private moment
i freeze at the door
stagger towards the body
kiss the cheeks, caress the hair

-23-
artifacts of pride
swedish-american pin
a patch of rainbow
the act-up pink triangle
his leather cap, airline wings

-24-
seven-hour wake
mother stands glued by my side
flight attendants flock
our kin, friends, & support group
sigh with relief "he looks good"

-25-
check from time to time
expecting him to arise
such a simple wish
amidst these wreaths & bouquets
he lies there in surreal peace

saturday, april 3, 1993

-26-
opening prayer
millieana, macieo, sheila
& hakan share thoughts
walter reads verse; willie sings
i, the control queen, emcee

-27-
ninth avenue east
corner of twenty-second
below our terrace
where the gay flag flies defiant
the hearse & our limos pause

-28-
spring-shower drizzle
we huddle round the dug grave
flowers & farewells
eyes cloud while we hug to watch
the descending casket rest

-29-
hakan & i smile
smell each other out then talk
i show him the will
sole beneficiary, but
i promise to split proceeds

-30-
at chic aquavit
fondly toast our love for him
memories flare back
i stare at that corner where
for his fiftieth, we dined

sunday, april 4, 1993

-31-
toss, twist, turn till dawn
t.v. keeps me company
cuddling the pillows
i slide to his side, dreaming
of his ass as i jerk off

-32-
radio gospel show
a choir belts out its soul
with amazing grace
i unpack his duffel bag
all items prized like relics

-33-
tracing back crossroads
soothed by cassettes of our songs
i roam chelsea streets
his voice guides my memory
to the corner where we met

-34-
this broken-fence pier
our favorite place besides home
same spot where we've curled
through twelve springs,
Summers,& falls
blessed in one another's arms

-35-
city in crisis
i sweep the view from the roof
"why am i alive"
shooting star, quick, make a wish
blurt it out "go away, aids"

No More Metaphors [Part One]

(Obituary printed in newspapers & memorial service program)

Jan Urban Holmgren, 53, died of AIDS at NYU Medical Center on March 29, 1993, in the arms of his life-partner Yves F. Lubin, also known as Assotto Saint.

Middle child of the late Gunda & Wolger Holmgren, Jan was born in Alno, Sweden, on April 25, 1939. He was also predeceased by his sister Berit Naslund.

After completing his tour of duty in the Swedish Army, his college education, & musical studies in Sweden, Jan left for the United States in 1965, looking for adventure.

A flight attendant for 25 years with American Airlines, Jan had won many professional awards. He traveled all over the world & was especially fond of Egypt.

Jan & Yves fell in love on November 9, 1980; the same week that the Reagan-Bush-SHIT government was first elected to the White House with its right-wing politics of greed, prejudice, & stupidity. As gay activists, they had both vowed never to succumb to AIDS during a Republican administration.

Soon after they met, they began their professional musical partnership. Jan composed the scores for their acclaimed theater pieces on gay black life, most notably *New Love Song, Risin' to the Love We Need, & Black Fag.* Their HI-NRG song "Forever Gay," was released on the CD/cassette *Feeding the Flame* by Flying Fish Records in 1990. A CD/cassette of some of their musical collaborations will be released next year.

Besides his life-partner, Jan is survived by his brothers Borje, Staffan, & Hakan Holmgren; his sisters-in-law: Anne-Marie, Gunhild, & Anne-Marie Holmgren; many nieces, nephews, & family members—all of Sweden; Yves's mother, Marie Lubin, & her family, who welcomed Jan as one of their own.

Jan also leaves behind, throughout the United States & Sweden, devoted longtime friends: Leif Ahlgren, Macieo Anderson, Millieana Boulton, Sheila Guertin, Hugo Person, Bruce Sokol, Frankie Tucker, & Aaron Woodruff, and many coworkers & friends who will always remember his sweet smile.

Join one million people on Jan's birthday, April 25, 1993, at the March on Washington for Lesbian, Gay & Bi Equal Rights & Liberation in Washington, D.C. Contact the National Office at 1012 14th Street, N.W., 7th Floor, Washington, D.C. 1-800-832-2889. A panel quilt in Jan's honor & memory will be delivered that day to the Names Project.

The March on Washington

from championing

those dying

of a virus

our government

neglects

to do much about

to fighting

for the right

of those who wish

to serve & die

for our country

the queer movement

refocuses itself

with a million of us

wishfully thinking

we've finally

"arrived" in a town

of backstabbers

even on blinding days

of sunshine

No More Metaphors [Part Two]

(Note delivered to the Names Project with a panel quilt of 4/24/1993)

I made this quilt for my 13-year life-partner, Jan Urban Holmgren. He was my Jan & my man. Born in Alno, Sweden, on April 25, 1939, he died in my arms on March 29, 1993. We both found out in late 1987 that we were HIV-positive. Jan came down with full-blown AIDS in early 1990. I came down with full-blown AIDS in late 1991. Yes, it is a strange phenomenon when both life-partners in a relationship are fatally ill.

Besides being a flight attendant with American Airlines for 25 years, Jan composed the scores for all of our acclaimed theater pieces on gay black life, most notably, *New Love Song, Risin' to the Love We Need, & Black Fag.* Our HI-NRG song, "Forever Gay," was released on the CD/cassette *Feeding the Flame* by Flying Fish Records.

Our pictures appeared in the pages of many national & local lesbian & gay magazines. We even graced some covers. We were a "hot" couple.

In many ways, our relationship symbolized how common ground can be found in "difference." Jan was 53 when he died. I am 35. Jan was white. I am black. Jan was born in Sweden. I am from Haiti. Jan believed in God. I don't. The list goes on & on; but we shared similar taste in music, exotic cuisine, traveling, political activism, & sexuality. We loved going to leather bars. We also loved the New York Knicks basketball team, our terrace in spring & summertime, soap operas, The Today Show, & our friends. We were committed & devoted to each other. I will always carry Jan's love in my heart. Because of my disbelief in God & a spiritual after-life, it gives me great pleasure to know that at least we will be physically reunited in the same grave at The Evergreens Cemetery in Brooklyn, NY.

I apologize for writing this letter by hand on yellow pad.

Enclosed is a copy of the memorial program for Jan's funeral service & the memorial card. The quilt was designed, cut, & pasted by me. My mother sewed it. The Names Project is such an important enterprise.

As long as AIDS continues to devastate, unfold it.

After the Parade & the Parties

in memoriam ortez alderson: national aids activist

a certain despair chills the d.c. air the morning after
elias sparks the sparse crowd with his speech & braids
at this civil disobedience i'll be arrested in jan's memory

half a decade after act-up exploded at the last march
so many busted on the steps of the supreme court
national aids activism is losing its steam & what a toll

1,000,000 infected throughout the united states
170,000 dead in this holocaust but the beat goes on
300 die-hard fools chant we'll never be silent again

47 block traffic near the capitol then dragged kicking
5 hours handcuffed tight by ever-watchful gloved cops
1 room of disillusion & where could larry kramer be

No More Metaphors [Part Three]

(Statement delivered at the Superior Court of
the District of Columbia on 4/28/93)

Your Honor, I am very grateful for the chance to make this statement
to the Court on why I felt it was necessary to block traffic on the
Capitol grounds. It resulted in my arrest, along with 46 other people,
on obstructing & impeding charges. The subject of the demonstration, as you well know, concerned health care.

I know something about health care on a professional level.
From July 1978, I worked for the New York City Health & Hospitals
Corporation until my pensioned retirement in October 1991, due to
AIDS-related disability.

I also know a lot more about health care on a personal level.
Since April 1983—an entire decade now—I have taken care of
my closest friends: Counsel Wright, Jose Caballero, Dr. Michael
Evans (aka M. E. Fuller). Redvers JeanMarie & David Frechette. I
have also taken care of my dear 13-year life-partner, Jan Urban
Holmgren. They have all died of AIDS. Jan died on March 29, 1993,
a month to the day tomorrow. No word could describe the helplessness, violation, & hopelessness that I felt as I watched him take
his last breaths. I would have given my own life if that could have
saved his.

I want to mention that I have also lost to AIDS many other close
friends who lived outside of New York City, hundreds of acquaintances all over the world, & 21 neighbors in my building on West
22nd Street in New York City. I have watched all of them disinte-
grate—some faster than others. Many lost their jobs, apartments,
belongings, friends, families, self-control, good looks, minds, & of
course, their faith.

In March 1990, I spent five days & nights with my life-partner, I
repeat FIVE DAYS & NIGHTS, in the Emergency Room of NYU Medical
Center, waiting for a bed on a medical ward to become available for

Jan. NYU Medical Center is one of the most prestigious institutions in the world & our affiliated doctors number among the best.

Three years later, in March 1993, I again spent five days & nights with my life-partner in the same Emergency Room, waiting for a bed on a medical ward to become available for Jan. Besides a few cosmetic changes here & there, nothing had much changed. Business as usual. This waiting game is a crying shame.

Your Honor, my life-partner & I had a combined income of $85,000. We were hardworking, tax-paying, & law-abiding. We were both foreigners—Jan was born in Sweden, & I was born in Haiti— who cherished the concept of the American Dream. Jan & I had very good medical insurance, which covered us for the rest of our lives. We both strongly believed that every individual in this country, no matter what socio-economic background he or she belonged to, deserves access to the best health care.

My illegal yet constitutional action this past Monday morning, to which I unashamedly plead guilty, was done on behalf of all the HIV-positive Haitians, who have been granted political asylum in the United States, but are being detained unlawfully & immorally at Guantanamo Bay. It was done of behalf of my late activist friend Ortez Alderson. It was done on behalf of my life-partner, Jan Urban Holmgren.

May the memory of their suffering, due to the inadequacy, greed, & stupidity of bureaucrats, finally bring much-needed transformation to our health care system. May it have helped to save my own life.

So, I hope.

The Loss of Faith

summon all your shrinking strength
so you won't lapse into a depression

try to keep emotions checked tight
midst the shell-shocked chaos of loss

you miss your lover's fjord-icy eyes
when shivering once more in desire

you would circle his chest with kiss
to surrender to wonders only yours

every day you stare at photographs
which flesh out bold blood-memories

echoes of a daily vow that together
you could stymie an insidious virus

blinded in a fog alone you forge on
but this is not the road to recovery

what faith can you now keep fueled
you're not scared of death just sad

No Symbols

"Questions long forgotten
What we've become has no name"
—Redvers JeanMarie

what we've become now has names

deceased & survivor

questions not forgotten

you left while i live to tell

so far you failed to return

as a vision of loveliness

on my birthday

the first of each year

your birthday

as mutually promised

i've waited

redvers, is there nothing to report

nothing to know about death

each one of us comes to terms

with this truth

plain like a curse

simple as nothing

else in life

The Queen's Etiquette

not some one-night stand
he is my faith, i his trust
till death do us part
so we had told a world where
envy is epidemic

***

a phone call, a card
even a small flowerpot
could have eased my grief
i say & watch blushing friends
wish that i too would drop dead

***

though i'm not gone yet
dissing queens dish dirt on me
it's all over town
k.s. inside that foul mouth
the bitch will have to shut up

Going Home Celebration

for donald woods

donald
the spectacle of your funeral
was a wake-up call from the dead
but history religiously repeats its travesty
in lunatic denial of an epidemic that decimates us
gay black men/

1.
anguish in the blood i arrive
skeptical after the obituary stated you died
of a heart attack which almost gave me one/
embracing at the door i search for more familiar faces
many like mine with tell-tale signs of dire times/
filing down the aisles we wink & wave/
nowadays in a world asunder
we often gather for farewells to beloved brothers like you
tongues heavy with laments & polemics of rage/

2.
weighted in tradition the service proceeds/
just one friend is lucky to participate through a solo
that rocks the stifling standing-room-only church/
two ladies share some rubbish about heaven & hell/
the eulogy recalls achievements & civil rights struggles
except for Other Countries cofounded closest to your heart/
this hour when our collective strength is tested
not one of your poems is read aloud to sustain us/

3.

some friends walk out as others hold each other tight/
some shake their heads as others shut their eyes/
duty calling across the church
i count the last beats of a recorded hymn/
then my feet whisk me to the pulpit like wings/
my breast pocket holds the deed to the plot i offered/
if anyone tries to stop me i'll fly out it/
i soar like an archangel summoning those wishing
to avenge your censored queer legacy

to stand up together to little old ladies in white dresses
fanning lies with cries of "save them, jesus"/
to stand up together to a pompous minister who under his breath
damned us for mass-invading his holy territory/
to stand up together to many dressed-to-kill family members
ready but unable to break our balls with their bibles/
to stand up together to a bewildered father needing a stiff drink
as he comes to grips with his son's faggotry/
to stand up together to a desperate mother who must safely deliver
to paradise her baby closeted in a pandora's box coffin/

Ironical Twist

for rodney dildy

no matter how numb i get
grieving many friends in such short span
it heartens me to hold my own candlelight memorials
the loss is not just some c.d.c. statistic but he flares again
through flaming flashbacks

one more gay black man dies
of aids & it had to be you rodney dildy
one more contributor to *The Road Before Us*
who does not survive all odds to craft poetry as he curses
dentures & social security

o brother of my crucibles
harnessing fears i cringe with guilt
wondering what's so fabulous about these gay nineties
recalling bacchanals when under crystal balls we all chanted
won't you take me to heaven

Devils in America

I was born on all angels day
but throughout my life
i've been a bitch out of hell/
don't nobody show up at my funeral
to call me nice or some shit like that/
save it for turncoat cocksuckers
who on their deathbeds
open their mouths wide to claim god/

though christianity befuddles me
i'm amazed at how it enslaves
the gay african-amercian community/
lately i've wished there's such a thing
as the almighty 'cause on judgment day
i'd unload a few choice words:

hey omniscient you
do you feel proud with so much
madness committed in your name/
hey omnipotent you
ain't you got nothing better to do
than making folks suffer/
hey omnipresent you
do you remember my lovers & I buttfuck/
go screw yourself
asshole of the universe/
can I get a witness/

Every Soul Is a Circus

again in a halloween parade life's a masquerade
she's gotta realize her fantasy & fantasize her reality

amidst this moving jungle of hunchbacked ghouls
there's a six-foot-four freak here but don't be scared

fierceness personified watch her strut her stuff
you just know she's walked the walk before

that she wears black from veiled head to painted toes
some understand as the decade's fashion statement

never guessing the queen's still in serious mourning
while forty-eight hours later on all souls' day

in banjeeboy getup she'll drag herself to the cemetery
clutching the reddest roses for her lover's grave

The Language of Dust

"From grave to grave
I carry my loyalty to you."
—Essex Hemphill

where
do you find
strength
to climb
down the hill
to your lover's
grave

what
do you bring
but thirteen years
of memories/

how do you deal
with his death
when your gasps
loom
in the autumn air
like circling crows
spasms rock
your body
like squirrels
shake the scarlet oak
& purple dogwood
branches
while through the buzz
of a helicopter
the roar
of an elevated train

the firecracker thunder
of a buddhist service
one can still hear

your sobs
over & over
utter his name/

jan
my jan
even blindfolded
I would find my way
to you
around this
evergreen cemetery

I gaze at
the engraved picture/
I outline
the entwined hearts/
I smooth out
the act-up triangle/

the musical notes
float high
on each side
of your viking name
along with dates of birth
& recent death/
poetry books

flap bold
on each side
of my voodoo pseudonym

birth name & date
open-ended/

I smile at
the "nuclear lovers" epitaph/
I sit on
the grass grateful

I will rest
not soon enough
right here
above you
in the shadow
of the trade center
towering
in the distance/

years ago
after we found out
our status
I begged you
to be buried
with me
because I don't believe
in the foolishness
of spiritual
afterlife

"the soul survives"
you insisted/

"prove it"
I demanded/

"man is the only creature
known to bury its dead"
you persisted/

"should we act
like dogs & swine"
I contended/

"manhattan queens
why should we be buried
of all places in brooklyn"
you retorted/

as usual
my patience thinned fast/
hysterical I screamed
if you died before me
I could not carry out
your wish to be
cremated/

at first
you laughed
that you would
outlast me
then guessing
the improbability
you lashed back
that I always need
to have things my way

threatening
to replace me
as your executor/

114

hurt
I held you hard
as you tried
to break away
from my embrace
while cross my heart
I swore
to do right by you/

there was this masochist
ex-priest
who after his lover's
cremation
adding a dash of ash
to the dough
every Sunday baked a batch
of peanut butter cookies
as he listened to mass
on the radio/

with no more communion
to down as morning pick-me-ups
to sweeten afternoon naps
to soothe nightmares
he dressed in a harness
knelt in the bathtub
slashed his wrists letting
his blood drop
in the urn
while on the cd
callas repeatedly sobbed
"vissi d'arte vissi d'amore"/

drama queen
he reminded me
of something
I would do
like that midday
in summer
I freaked
pulled out my dick
jerked off quick
on the geraniums
over the grave/

I also remember
during my second hospitalization
we watched
this television report
on greedy companies
that cremated corpses
together
& handed families
the wrong remains/

open-mouth shaken
you paced the room
we shared in co-op care/
laid down with p.c.p.
my throat got tight/

then last year
in the candlelight glow
of a swedish meatballs
haitian rice & beans
anniversary dinner
capped with entenmann's eclairs

you affirmed to be buried with me
would honor our relationship/

that night
we curled
into each other
aware
one of us
would leave roses
tears & kisses
on our tombstone
the next november 9th/

Mater Dolorosa

this thanksgiving night i am blessed to be with you mother/
the guests gone, the dishes done, leftovers stored, we recline
on your sofa for the late news: a world forever in disarray/

quickly you doze off & i wish you the sweetest dreams/
a sudden guilt chills me to look back on the tumult of our past
where do i start; how do i start; why should i start/

born out of wedlock in your high-profile political family/
not knowing who my father was & feeling abandoned
in aunt marcelle's care while you lived abroad/

coming out flaming queen soon after i joined you in this country
barely in my teens, disco dancing, dropping premed to become a
dancer/you were not amused & i had to move out on my own

aids strikes, look, my name is on the new york times' front page/
cbs, cable, a film, speeches, essays—my diagnosis a whirlwind/
you beg me to "take it easy" to which i snap back "in my grave"/

racing against the clock i finally pen this poem to thank you
for giving me life & supporting me through my dying/
carry it in your breath, breasts, & blood as a cure for our ills/

Heart & Soul

to essex hemphill

every day
every time i leave my house
everywhere i go
i pin on my knapsack
twin petal-small flags
to which my allegiance is pledged
whole

these flags are not monkeys on my back
i carry them as a coat of arms
mantles of double brotherhood
they shield like second skin
to drape my dreams

one floats rainbow
the other wings tricolor
both bold with movement
i am not ashamed
of what they stand for
when their meaning is
questioned

these flags are not chips on my shoulders
i carry them as beauty spots
markings of double brotherhood
they shine like mirror beads
to reflect prejudice

one unfurls the future of the queer nation
the other salutes african ancestors

both wave s.o.s. signals
i am not afraid
to stand my ground
when their beauty is
challenged

these flags are not crossbones on my life
i carry them as amulets
emblems of double brotherhood
they spellbind like stars
to stripe america

glory
that becomes me in tribal rituals
& battle against bigots
i have honored with my blood
everywhere i go
every time i leave my house
every day

Leave or Die

next time
under cover of darkness
or high noon

someone shouts "fuckin' faggot"
fists fly

out of your pocket
unclasp a safety pin
prick your finger quick

blood spurts
queerly ask "lookin' for aids"

dare stand brave
remember this land is home
aim free

Uncollected Poems

Early on Easter Sunday

for richard washington

early on easter sunday
you call
to offer the friend some faith
you hope
when the grandmother answers
you dread
ricky's no longer with us
you hear
what in god's name does that mean
you ask

Does the Buck Stop Here

her desert storm army assignment accomplished
a purple heart twinkles on her fatigues' lapels
this redneck crew cut united states soldier
in spit-shining boots hobbles off a helicopter

jesse helms-country sunset bleeds old glory waved
on april fool's when national fervor heats up
our anthem which a band pumps for the parade
four network cameras' flash catch all that panache

bright-eyed cute, dimples, and sunday suit
yellow bow tie flowering his fresh-pressed shirt
screaming, "mommy" whom he had missed for months
a lad loosens his grandmother's tight grip

rushing up, limping down a ramp, child and mom
reunite with hug, kisses, tears; so america applauds
the world watches a wet-eyed anchorman ask: "ma'am
can you tell us how you will celebrate tonight?"

"i reckon that after i tuck my little timmy in bed
round midnight, i'm gonna turn on my cd player
then this mother here gonna finally chill out
with a nice bubble bath and a 46-ounce bud bottle

"listen to ms. k.d. lang sing those sweet lips out
while i be soaking and stroking all night long"
she says directly to the camera then winks off
as she pats the shocked reporter's shoulder

"all power to you, sister," i shout back
heading for the fridge to pop me a pepsi
and give my mind a sweet break from this
broadcast obsessed with mid-east madness

"but where's the husband?" i ask myself
"disappeared? divorced? dead? anybody?
need there be a man in that household?"
i laugh off my questions and presumptions

glad she's back "home" where freedom is not
some discriminating taste no woman savors
like in the land she supposedly just helped
to liberate for a so-called new world order

Old Forms/New Norms

two i.v. bags hang
like masks on a totem pole
shrunk of solution
one's dried up while fluids full
another drips life

AIDS Talk

"what's your lover in for?"
bill asks bob in the cafeteria
as he bites his toast

bob chews his cereals carefully
& answers "cancer" then he asks
"how about yours?"

"pneumonia" bill coughs up
gulps grapefruit juice then asks
"what kind of cancer?"

bob frowns then whispers "k.s."
as he spoons milk to his lips
he asks bill "p.c.p.?"

N.Y.U. Hospital
Coop Care
Cafeteria

Evidence

ticking in darkness, thoughts cough
the long night mires memory
howls gristle virus-spittle
lave scathes
the ground it waits; the ground it wants

gay boys stricken
again then again & again
black men broken
again then again & again
best friends taken
again then again & again

stumble to the bathroom
sit on the hard bowl
blot out the blurs
wash your hands quickly
splash water all over face
brush your tongue slowly
flush down all residue
smile at the
stop for a sudden rush
crack up the frosted window

gay boys stricken
again then again & again
black men broken
again then again & again
best friends taken
again then again & again

arms folded around your chest
the dawn draws to its promise
are you worthy of this sunrise
bursts of light echo
witness, you are graced to bear

The Impossible Black Homosexual
[OR Fifty Ways to Become One]

(after a poem called "Women" by Nicanor Parra and
after a poem called "Men" by Erica Jong)

the impossible black homosexual

the one whose father's feelings are chiseled in steel

the one whose mother should have considered an abortion

        a serious option

the one who is a case of b.p.n.c.

        (bad prenatal care)

the one who runs his life on c.p.t.

        (colored people time)

the one who falsified his birthdate

        but couldn't change his fate

the one who changed his name

        still has no fame

the one who was born in the boondocks of haiti

        but often pretends to be french canadian

        on the party phone sex lines

the one who calls at all hours

        when he needs you

the one who seldom calls

        but always just thinking of you

        each time you call

the one you call "miss thing"

the one who calls himself "madame thing"

the one who can be "sweet thing"

the one who will too often stop at nothing

the one who's more illusionist than pan the magician

        if you are not his type

the one with more pretentious agendas

        than the united states congress

        in session

in an election year
the one who regularly breakfasts on baldwin
                    porno videos & bananas with granola
the one who eats shit
                    every weekday from nine to five
the one who treats you as shit
                    every friday night until last call for a cock
the one who once got crabs for christmas
                    (not the kind you eat either)
the one who named his trio of dildoes
                    dinge, mandingo & [ ]
the one padded with the 7-1/2 inch ad
the one who clones & pumps iron
the one whose biggest childhood fantasy was to dress women
the one whose adult reality is often to dress up as a woman
the one who when he was fourteen
                    did it with a girl
                    then he lived in brooklyn
the one who when he was fifteen
                    did it with old men in movie theaters
                    then he lived in queens
the one who when he was sixteen
                    did it with the driver in the back of a bus
                    then he lived in queens
the one who when he was seventeen
                    did it with a uniformed cop in a subway tearoom
                    then he lived in queens
the one who since he was eighteen
                    did it north south east & west of the big apple
the one whose spirits at times drive him a bit too spirited
                    all over the world
the one with the white lover whom he met in a backroom bar
                    white lover twenty years his senior
                    white lover he's lived with for over a decade

the one who in the midst of this crisis
                    still celebrates vicious officious cocks
the one who yells at his white tricks
                    "i'm gonna fuck you with this big black dick"
the one who yells at his black tricks
                    "yeah, fuck me with that big black dick"
the one who even after extended one-night stands
                    always crawls back to his nuclear lovers' nest
                    in chelsea
the one who on the day he was tested for hiv
                    seduced his doctor who was also his lover's
the one who's p.i.s.d.
                    (person with immune system disorder)
the one who acts up in rainbow politics
the one who acts out with purple prose
the one who acts now in front of you
the one, yes, this one
                    you all know who he is
                    while he's trying to figure that out
the one who keeps putting on more masks
                    yet will never stop pulling down
                    his jockstrap
the one who keeps burying his best friends
                    & each time whispers
                    "sorry it's you but glad it ain't me"
the one who doesn't want to deal with death
                    but death will probably deal with him
                    much sooner than later
the one who keeps thinking about heaven
                    & knows he ain't heading there
                    "there's no there, there"
the one who threatens to reincarnate
                    as either the second coming or an atom bomb
                    (they will both fuck you over)

the one who on the day he naturalized as an american citizen
                 sat naked on the current president's picture
                 & after he was finished
                 called the performance "bushshit"
the one who for 365 days out of the year is
                 the impossible black homosexual
all these faces facets & phases
out of my mind will not drive me
i know their kind
bless them all
only too well

Strike Up Music

strike up music
music that'll take me out of the middle of this tunnel
where i've been looking for the moon since high noon

strike up music
music to get me high on a star-ship comet
six flying saucers blaze at my trail
eighteen million eyes 3-D my move out
of new york city into the world
ain't no magic below
america, what kind of bad card did we draw

strike up music
music & please hold back those tears
bernard goetz, I got no time to hear bullets ricochet
& i'm way past pelham bay parkway
so i don't have to make sense outta everybody's philosophy
scrawled on all walls
whatever it is
i leave you my very best wishes
gotta go about my business
see & feel nothing earthy

strike up music
planet mars
planet mars are you listening
hey pluto
venus can we talk
information . . . .

Curse

for michael griffith

I.

epithets baseball bats iron tire shatter
the late night's muteness
& a black man beseeches his god
not to let him fall on calvary
but mercury flashes down pluto's summon
away from america
may he discover her more & more

II.

i shake off the nightmare's sweat
to cleanse my soul
i shake it off to cleanse history
cold sweat this water is no blessing
& the rage in me climbs out
to free the sun
in our sky of clouds

Body Beautiful

you are the body beautiful
hot-shot cosmic vision quite earthly
look at these curled triceps
crunch-beast belly
squat steel legs
stretched diamond calves

you are the body beautiful
with the ardor, vigor, & splendor
ready for aerobic endeavors
which row motions into emotions
break taboos
make new genres

you are the body beautiful
not just the come on
but my mr. dreams for real
& i'm always willing
to do a donkey calf raise
with you partner

I Once Asked a Trick

i once asked a trick if he had a religion
puzzled, he answered, "i'm a free man"

i then asked him if he had a lover
quickly, he answered, "i'm free, man"

Blessings

"are you brothers"
that gentle guide of almond lips
whispered deep
into the night with hashish thick
while high on camels we roamed
that desert of temples tombs & two-star hotels
one finger in & out of two others' circle
he stammered
you nodded
i laughed
we both choked out
"forever"

***

years later grateful
keys chains hankies hang out of your pockets
pearls from my ear
trusting togetherness
your voice of fugues & my pen which paints hell
crossing barriers states borders
i do dream to grow old beside you
swap late night florida backyard stories
cherishing smiles of those who passed along
in the family
that we survived all odds
to cuss our social security dentures & memory

Deja Vu

for michael

bricks knots shards in my chest
i stagger search then knock
bearing garland of weeklies wafers & daisies
so soon at this entrance again
waving he barely whispers
i too can't breathe

Jan Saw a Blind Man

jan saw a blind man/ all smiles in the sun/ the prayers of our mothers/
he saw him and wondered what he saw in the darkness/
he could witness the world was unhappy/ my fingers caked with cum
    i begin my diary/
jan closed his eyes/ time represents itself/ the polemics of rage & riots
the little sentimental moments & things that break you apart/
never hold him close as he holds me/ i live in a society/
    enjoy fantasies turn into realities
never to watch him smile as i whisper softly in his ears that i love him
never to feel his hands caress my face as he tells me you're so sweet and
    we kiss/
never to sit on our terrace with all the flowers/
finding him in the waiting room of the x-ray
talking to the haitian technician
who never thought i was haitian
(tell him about relationship/ i have aids)
two lives/ one partnership/
two hearts/ one love/ many sex partners/
one look/ one night/ one house/
one strength/ one piece/ one bed/ one dream/ one kiss/ one cover/
    one more time/
one window/ one crescent moon/ one virus one story line/ one decade/
    one grave/ one stone/one word: dead
there i was in the middle of the sistine chapel of all places right in the
    center underneath the creation
amidst all the noisy tourists
when suddenly i heard a voice from the beyond saying "cocks"
at first i didn't know what hit me/
after all, i was in the vatican (pope court with his cardinals/
and i laughed/ Michelangelo/ freak show for friends/ those who
    mistake diary entries for

poems/ a literature of memorials & treatments/ my tongue heavy
   with another lament/ is poetry possible in the plague/
sometimes when you're not getting something, you hail a vision everyday
but she's a nurse, she should be strong/
she's a mother too, she often reminds you
she's weakened—you still hate it
yes, it's the same mother you hit with both hands
clear skies of a sunday morning in fall
that hour when the sun barely risen
hangs like a halo/ discernible and not this bright blinding explosion
   of rays
calm and not so jittery as noon vibes/
the diatribe queen/ tears are necessary but not enough/
the human soul in xtremis
memorialize the dead & the dying/ trying to fight despair through
   the protest afforded by human imagination & capacity to
   confront/ incalculable suffering caused by that disease/
enduring power of art in the face of horror/
ortez, you gaze down at me piercingly each time i sit down at my desk/
ortez/ ortez alderson/ activist/ actor/ friend
the quilt/ it's my blood/ my disease/ it's my love/ my heart/ it's his death/
   it's my silence/ it's his midnight/ it's our hour/ it's his lips/ it's my
   grief/ it's our love/ it's our falling sky/ it's his ground/ it's my quilt/
   safety pins/ it's my tears/ it's his memories/ hold me/ i'm not strong/
   it's him/ it's me/ it's us/ dumping fistfuls of dirt in your grave/ don't be
   caught alone/ the river/ the clouds/ dilapidation/ disintegration/ sun
   breaking through sunset/ statue of liberty/ empire state building/ high
   tide/ circle line/ it's a sailboat/ jan's music & my memories/ the rose in
   the river/ wind chill/ forgot handkerchief/ sobbing into gloves/ petals
   breaking apart/ the new testament for my heart/ the bill of rights for
   my mind/ all i want in my coffin/ human will & heart will triumph
never cared for the term lovers but used it expediently
significant others sounded significant
better-half and double brothers quite colloquial

companions connotated no sex

life-partners reflected the totality

a child draws shades on a morning sky, opens the window so that the cat
 can perch itself on the ledge/ a backyard of weeds & broken bottles/
 crushed dentures/ open eyes like this past valentine, celebrating our
 13th valentine, brought him 14 new red roses/

superstitious

are you brothers

that gentle guide of almond lips

whispered deep

into the hashish-thick night

while high on camels we roamed

the desert of temples tombs & two-star hotels

one finger in & out of two others' circle

he stammered, you nodded, i laughed

we both choked out "forever"

years later, grateful, i do dream to grow old beside you

swap late-night florida backyard stories

cherishing smiles of those who passed along

that we survived all odds

to cuss out social security, dentures & memory

moments that cemented our relationship

each one of us closing one of joe's eyes,

the temples of karnak, our beach in haiti

carrying three roses from the wreath

dumping fistfuls of dirt in your grave, not out of anger but as a finality

you hope that they will follow your wishes, put on your long black gloves,
 the drop earrings, the lipstick kente cloth scarf, mahogany coffin

"it's you" he mutters as i put my hands over his face

your hands are so cold and dry he says then holds them and kisses them,
 "i still love you" he mutters & kisses them

144

Let Me See the City I Love So Much

on the roof let me see the city i love so much in nighttime
let me soak up the view one more time
you became superhuman trying to live up to your promise
crouched on two chairs where people like the old man whom the nurse
   asked how come you never married but she and you guessed that he
   was gay/ the shit/
one eye open, the other closed
suction him up, he cries, i hold his hand
cover his head with kisses/ i will not outlive him long/ i don't believe in
   god/ i don't believe in an afterlife/ jan lives in our memories & in my
   broken heart
gazing upward, his mouth open with a song you can't hear
there's the window, to grab him & fly out/ angels in america
now & then i have this vision of being caught at the crossroads
of a city in darkness, cool as hope and facing me in huge flames hot as
   despair with lots of possibilities/ looking back to soak it one more time
then marching straight to hell
get up in the cold, marching & shouting through downtown streets
once a year, in an orgy of self-congratulatory bullshit, they meet for
   big business
writing about my diagnosis, dying & death as if i will
   survive through thoughts
black & white, action failed, my politics failed, industry to greed
vestiges of sanity & pride, the challenge verifies our need
last hope the ground with your prints
this came out of me
the will will outlast my life on earth
capable of analysis, above average
something they'll learn, not enough to fight the enemy/
as if writing clears the fog of questions away

therapy, release, sanity before dementia sets in & all common
    sense vanishes
this will trick the virus that wants to wipe all traces
it starts with your body, job strength
something to cling on to, libido,
down to nothing, vegetable
something others will remember you by
desire does not diminish
it is fueled by time
every other aids poem is a eulogy
the goddamn truth is that people die every day
while mothers are birthing babies
i was born on all angels day
writing about aids to keep friends' names alive
tripping and falling, rebounding
the world would have gotten aids with or without reagan
writing about aids as retribution to unearth bits of memories
writing is an afterthought/ it is passive
each holocaust has its heroes & its victims & its territory
& you want laughter/ it's never the same/
    the car crash with its marks & wreckage
images that can translate horror in magical translation
nothing special about aids or hiv illness
every nuance of horror documented/ hieroglyphs to be deciphered
archives/ what made him tick/ something happened/ a movement
    out of nowhere/
like a doctor's charts/
yes, the muthah-fuckah & i met on November 9, 1980 around 11:00 P.M.
Yes, we were life partners going into our 13th year together
yes, the muthah-fuckah died in my arms on March 29, 1993
    around 11:15 P.M.
yes, our love will last forever
words that come back to haunt
actions when you failed each other

when you both threw words like darts
his moustache, his hands, his forehead
the feel of his ears, the bridge of his nose, linking fingers
three months after his death
felice who has gone through the same loss said it will take years
i sit on the bench facing the grave and look back
sometimes i lay on the bench
& wake up almost startled as if i hear his voice calling me
i imagine that i see him standing here with a quizzical smile
feelings my therapist says/ feelings i want to hear all bout your feelings/
i don't want no report of things that happened/
sometimes, next to him, i jerk off
i miss him, his lips, his hole, his cock, his balls in my mouth
then he wakes up & holds me
yes i met the mutha-fuckah on 11/9/80 around 11:00 P.M.
yes we were life-partners moving into our 13th year together
yes the mutha-fuckah died in my arms 3/29/93 around 11:15 P.M.
yes our love will last forever
our last public performance together
singing forever saying goodbye to the community
lying on the mall grass by myself/ clutching a piece of jan/
moving away from the movement
listening to speaker after speaker/ took off my doc martens/ no rage
business as usual/ cute young sailors
do they remember matlovich
this is the picture to present
is poetry possible in an epidemic
does it save lives
jan vomiting at United AIDS Day/ my mother/ he's holding a sign
    "Mr. President Help me I have AIDS"/ take him home/ he can't walk
you become superhuman trying to keep him alive/
    trying to live up to your promise
crouched on 2 chairs/ one eye open, the other closed
suction him up/ he cries/ i hold his hand/ cover his head with kisses

gazing upward/ his mouth open with a song we can't hear/there's the
    window/ to grab him & fly out/ angels in america/
    the heat of desperate men
in the comfort that they have helped to save you/ the fear of being alone/
but nothing helped/ my fingers caked with cum i begin my diary/
i was born in the land of drums (never stop beating)
1960 (gayness)
1970 (blackness) angela davis poster/ bobby seale/ afro pick
1980 (love/interracial)
1990 (aids)
2000 (what)
i who killed god in our family/ barely breathing from bouts of pneumocystis
see the fingers splay/ losing our strength
gunda died today/ mission accomplished/ here in sundsvall/

Uncollected Song Lyrics

The ACT UP Song

too young
let us not fall like cattle
to redeem america's plaguing prejudices
let us act up
fight back
fight aids

aids-aids-aids
aids-aids-aids

the word is buzzing at our door
try to find places to hide
gay or straight, rich & poor
not even time on our side
the human race must find a way
come together, break down the walls
but do we know the price we pay
say nothing, nothing at all

no-no-no-no
no-no-no-no
silence = death
death-death
death-death

act up
take a stand & fight back
act up
take a stand & fight aids
act up
take a stand & fight back

act up
take a stand & fight aids

you gotta give me an "a"
you gotta give me a "c"
you gotta give me a "t"
you gotta give me a "u"
you gotta give me a "p"
i gotta act up
you gotta act up
we gotta act up

where was george
read-my-lips
bushshit
bushshit

where was george
read-my-lips
bushshit
bushshit

152

Touch

i always wished to find a man for whom i'll care
                                   with whom i'll share
i always wished to feel his touch so soft & fair
                                   the kind so rare

touch is what i want
touch is what i need
touch me, be with me
everywhere

i searched so long, i have been lost & unaware
                                   you were right there
now that i found you, i am not scared, my soul i bare
                                   touch you i dare

touch is what I want
touch is what I need
touch me, be with me
everywhere

touch me
oh be with me
touch me, be with me
everywhere

Galiens

strangers once from different lands
we came here holding dreams
same old song but a different band
our history is a travesty
to live free & be happy
as gay men that's where we stand
let's all start to redeem our dreams
the future lays right in our hands

galiens making connections
galiens setting foundations
we are men loving men
galiens making connections
galiens setting foundations
we are men loving men

america, land of the free
america, home of the brave

we are men loving men
we are men loving men
we are men loving men
we are men loving men

Forever Gay

black & white, red, brown, & yellow
butch or fem, one of a kind
jeans fit tight, & i am on the go
work out in gyms, body's my pride

cruise at night, trip, or disco
s & m, taste is refined
outta sight, over the rainbow
looking for dreams outta your mind
i'm outta your mind

black-white-red-brown-yellow
black-white-red-brown-yellow

living my life my way
living from day-to-day
no matter what you say
i'm gonna stay forever gay
forever gay

we're here
we're queer
we're fabulous
get used to it
gay-gay-gay is a happy word

living my life my way
living from day-to-day
no matter what you say
i'm gonna stay forever gay
forever gay

earth & air, fire & water
spirits still up, states of desire
everywhere, called the front runner
just won't stop till i get higher
till i get higher

life-liberty-happiness
we hold these truths to be self-evident
all men are created equal
life-liberty-happiness
we hold these truths to be self-evident
but all men are not created equal

we're here-we're queer-we're fabulous-get used to it
we're here-we're queer-we're fabulous-get used to it
we're here-we're queer-we're fabulous-get used to it
we're here-we're queer-we're fabulous-get used to it
gay-gay-gay is a happy word

living my life my way
living from day-to-day
no matter what you say
i'm gonna stay forever gay
forever gay

living my life my way
living from day-to-day
no matter what you say
i'm gonna stay forever gay
forever gay
forever gay
forever gay
forever gay
forever gay

Tears of Laughter

have you seen the rain fall
while the sunshine sparkles
have you seen the rain fall
like tears of laughter

running far away
running from it all
i slept one night in open air
when i woke up what i saw
made my day
it made my day

have you seen the rain fall
while the sunshine sparkles
have you seen the rain fall
like tears of laughter
like tears of laughter
like tears of laughter

Roller Coaster

love is like a roller coaster
going up & down
love, the universe's greatest wonder
once when we were riding wild & high
so high that we could reach the sky
i thought our world was infinite

love is like a roller coaster
going up & down
love, the universe's greatest wonder
now that we are tumbling rough & down
so down that we can kiss the ground
i see our world crash at our feet

go & find yourself all that you're missing
oh just do your thing & move around
maybe i'll be here if you should come back
maybe i'll have packed then hit the town

ro-ro-ro-ro roller coaster up & down
ro-ro-ro-ro roller coast round & round
we're rolling on
down

Fiction

Miss Thing/for marcia johnson

had you been driving on the west side highway by 10th street last thursday, you would have seen miss thing turning it out at 4:00 A.M./

long blond tresses sprigged with gold, plucked eyebrows, purple mascara around the eyes to make them look large & luminous, cheek- bones that won't quit, thick green flutters, chain-shaped silver pen- dants framing her coffee-colored full face, ruby reds & loads of rouge to hide the shaving marks, reeking of avon, she was bad/ the way she carried on waiting for a john, everyone could tell that she was a he/

caped in flawless purple satin splashed with gold beads & trimmed with black ostrich, she leaned her six-foot frame against the fire- alarm pole, looking so sexy in this hot pink dress, slit on both sides to the waist, sashed with a gigantic bow/

miss thing, she had seen such things in a copy of *Vogue* which she'd picked up from the garbage can in front of the Waverly/ for an entire week, she had slaved over the outfit/ the gold fringes & the paillettes were her own touch/ until that night, she hadn't had time to premiere it/

2 weeks ago, hustling in the manhattan plaza garage, a cop grabbed her right out of her lover's arms in the backseat of a '69 pinto/ he warned & let her beau go but whisked her to the queens's tank where some of the girlies waited months for a court date/ out of their bitter frustration fought with one another/

miss thing pleaded guilty each time she got busted/ that's how her record was so long & messed up/ she'd agree to serve a week or 10 days at rikers/ that was the sure way out/ after all, she had no sugar-daddy/ she couldn't get a sympathetic lawyer & those johns to whom she'd brought so much love, they were of no help/

she'd go to bars, strike up conversation with one of those too boozed up to hold his head straight/ the boy would gladly oblige; buy the lady a drink or 2/ she'd lull him outside with sweet talk, promises of good times/ no money deal just free love/ she'd walk him along deserted streets to some hot-spring hotel/ he'd feel good, leaning against her strong shoulders, talking, crying about marital troubles/ soon as he would smile, look at her through bleary eyes, she'd quickly pull out a blade & he'd say: "here . . . take everything/ leave me alone"/ she would & she'd make it back to the bar in time to slip a bill in the bartender's pocket/ she had to support a silicone & hormone treatment/ s.s.i. just wouldn't do/ she was no queen made up for the night/ drag was her life/ "honey," she'd tell you, "this shit's a trip!"

things weren't so easy/ good times were far away/ once, this puerto-rican dude picked her up down delancey/ after she showed him her tongue's delight (she was not like one of these high-mighty queens one finds at gg's who say: "do anything to me just don't touch my face," well, after she nearly passed out from so much talcum powder & so much brut, he wanted to take her the normal way/ to make her feel his big dick deep down like he had kept whispering/ lost in some fleeting fantasy she didn't realize what he was up to until he screamed: "maricon! maricon!" she saw her dainties & g-string at her feet/ she barely got out of the car after much struggling & biting when he shot her in the back/ the bullet passed through her stomach, leaving a scar/ for weeks at bellevue, she joked with the nurses about her two belly buttons/

a shimmy-here, a slimmer there, she advertised that stuff, casting come-on glances at the passing cars which caused church-going gals to pull up their windows fast & look the other way/ most of the guys though would do a double-dig/ one night, some poor slob crashed into a pole/

as she posed in the middle of the street, waiting to flag a car, she saw this crazy-looking white boy coming her way/ she took off her green spike pump fast, brandishing it in her right hand/ her left on her hip, cheeks sucked in, lips pushed out with a whistle, she stared straight at him, ready to strike/ he smiled, blew her a kiss while he walked by/

in the distance she thought she heard a siren/ cosmetic intuition she calls it/ she tried to run to the piers & fell in a puddle/ hopping on one sandal, she dragged herself behind a parked volkswagen as a paddy waggon whizzed by/ "i ain't garbage to be swept off the streets whenever some goddamn pig feels like it!" she yelled/ "the streets belong to the people and i am somebody/ next time you force me down on you, i'll bite it off/ no dough, no blow/"

she stood there 'til the siren sounded far away/ then, she sat on the edge of the boardwalk, all wrapped up in her cape, legs dangling in the air, smoking the last cigar from a pack this guard with whom she'd made it in jail, had given her/ he had been very nice, bringing her issues of *Ladies' Home Journal, Reader's Digest* & once, pictures of his old lady which miss thing had begged him for/ each time they'd gotten together, he had offered her 10 bucks which she had quickly refused, saying: "just tell me i'm better than her"/ he would and she knew he meant it/

she stared for a long time at her reflection in the water/ the wind blew unkind/ as she raised her head looking dead-ahead. she sang/

Hooked for Life

There were no tears. There was no time for tears that year. Just a tight knot in the pit of my chest where it hurts more each day. Yet, it had all come to this: a two-pound plastic bag filled with ash, bits of bones, fragments of teeth that didn't completely burn. It had all come too quickly.

It seems only yesterday, Riis Park bustled with laughter and WBLS blasted music everywhere. Beautiful bodies languished on the sand in colorful swimsuits. Volleyball players along with joggers ran up and down. Lifeguards whistled swimmers who strayed too far. Some vendors hawked pepsi and ice-cream sandwiches. Others hustled cheap cologne and fake gold bracelets. That day of wine and smiles, we were all walking on sunshine.

Next to me, on our "I LOVE NEW YORK" beach mat, dreads cascading down his head, Duke eased through his one hundred daily push-ups. Every inch of his six-foot muscular body glistened deliciously like honey. Many a passing glance sized him up but the dude was all mine and had been mine for ten years. He was so fine that I paid no attention to a spot on his left foot, right below his big toe; a spot, small, purple like the stain of a crushed grape.

Soon after, it multiplied like stars in early evening. Like buds on a tree in early spring, it multiplied all over his feet, his legs, up his ass, inside his intestines, all over his face, his neck, down his throat, inside his brains. For nine months of fever and wracking coughs, nine months of sweat and shaking chills, nine months of diarrhea and jerking spasms, it multiplied, wrenched him skinny like a spider: a body of pain.

"Sky, I don't understand this. I don't want to understand this," popped out of Duke as he came out of the anesthesia. "I'm sick of this hose in my nose. I'm sick of this tube in my dick, all these IVs in my arms. I'm sick of being strapped to this bed." He coughed out a scream.

"Easy, easy baby," I whispered, smoothing my gloved hand over his head, the side they hadn't shaved for the biopsy, glad he was starting trouble again. I bet he could see my smile behind the mask they had made me wear.

"I ain't joking. I am tired," he said. "I am really tired and I'd rather be dead."

"Sir Duke, don't you talk like that. You ain't gonna die. You're only thirty-one, you're too young to die. We gonna beat this shit," I kept repeating. "That's why I want you to come home where you belong. One month is too freaking long to stay cooped up in this room. This hospital food ain't fit for a dog. I'm gonna make you strong. We gonna cheat death, you hear me. Sky and Duke, hooked for life. Come on say it. Say it like we used to sing all the time. Say it."

"Sky," he muttered, "I'm gonna die."

"No!" I kept yelling in the corridor.

"Mr. Carter, calm down," the head nurse said as she rushed into Duke's room with another nurse.

"What's the number for the Administrator On Duty?" I asked this short Filipino nurse. "I want to take my lover home."

"Take him home, what do you mean?" she asked.

"I believe I'm speaking English. I said I want to take him home."

"But your friend is dying. The biopsy showed Kaposi's."

"You are killing him. You and all this hospital ain't doing shit for him. Idiots! You should be ashamed of yourselves."

"Stop it! Stop this nonsense right now and I mean it," the head nurse said to me as she walked back. "You ain't gonna come here in my ward and upset my staff. Is that understood?"

I kept quiet and looked past her as the Filipino nurse walked away.

"Mr. Carter, I'm still waiting for an answer."

"Yes," I shouted back and closed my eyes.

"You can do all the screaming you want, loud as you need but from now on, you do it outside. That's exactly where you should be carrying on in the first place. It's obvious to a duck that if enough of you homosexuals were acting up in the streets, those politicians would be taking you quite seriously and allocate much more money for research. I don't have to teach you history. You told me you was born in the South just like me, and brother, if most of us in the 1950s and 1960s didn't get into civil disobedience, march-ins, sit-ins, we would still be riding in the back of the bus."

"You should really talk, sister! Really! Like most black folks, you probably believe that we gays are getting just what we deserve."

"Now, that's way beneath you and I won't even bother to dignify that with an answer," she said as she started to walk away then turned back. "Better yet, look! Look around you. You see all these little cabinets outside those rooms. I don't have to tell you what's in those little cabinets or why they're standing outside those rooms, do I? Count them. Go ahead, count them. That's right, nine! Nine rooms with AIDS patients in a ward of seventeen beds. Nine! Eight young men and one young lady who's so demented, the poor thing don't even know her name. You think I like to see all this misery. You think it don't break my heart to be messed up in all this hopelessness. I don't like this. I'm telling you I don't like it one bit but all of us in this hospital are trying to do the very best we can under these circumstances. Unfortunately that ain't enough but Lord help us all. Now why don't you go get some rest. You'll be doing your friend and yourself a disservice if you continue this vigil. Come on sit. Sit down and drink some water." She filled a paper cup and put it to my lips. "It's alright," she said. "Honey, I understand," and she held me.

From then on, I wasted no time. Duke was too weak now, but in a week he could be home. He did consent after much convincing, insisting that I take down all twelve mirrors hanging on every single wall in the apartment. My indefinite leave of absence was approved quickly. Ever since I had told my co-workers about Duke's illness and why I had been so stressed, they've been wiping the unit's phone with alcohol. This year, they even asked me to bring vodka and gin to the Christmas party instead of my tasty fritters they used to love; at times saved some for their kids.

I took a bank loan; said it was for continuing education. I rented a wheelchair, a walker and a commode. I bought sheepskin pillows, a portable suction machine, a stand-up bed tray, hot water bottles, all kinds of medical supplies and bundles of paper towels. With coupons and Duke's food stamps, I stacked up the refrigerator. I vacuumed, dusted and waxed the parquet floor. I called on friends and neighbors to volunteer for chores. My sister Belzora, a retired registered nurse, said that she'd come up from Georgia. Instead of a hard narrow bed in a sterile room, Duke would die in the dignity and the beauty of his own home, on our big brass bed.

"Sir Duke, do you remember the first time we met at Peter Rabbit?" I asked him the night he came home as we sat on the living room sofa, his head resting on my chest.

"How could I forget? You and your bunch of loud friends were bitching at the bar, singing them ballads so off-key. Sky, you were stoned-drunk."

"I was not. I was just enjoying a nice Sunday soiree. Besides, you're the one who walked in them tight bell-bottom jeans and platform shoes, got everybody's hearts pumping and jumping. Child, you looked so good and when the d.j. played "Hooked for Life" I had to ask you to dance.

That night, we sang, even danced a bit. Two disco divas with ten years of memories: the trips, the parties, the steps, the orgies, laughter . . .

"Sky," he whispered as I tucked him in bed and kissed him good night, "I'm glad I'm home. I love you. Thanks for the good times."

Time was running out. Days went by. Duke made a will and named me executor of his estate. He couldn't get up or eat by himself. Belzora flew in like she had promised. She fixed all those deep-southern dishes Duke used to like but could hardly eat. He'd stare at the wall with a glazed far-away look, eyes sunken way back.

Nights went by. He gagged, choked and vomited. I helped him sit up and cough, massaged his back, washed him up, changed his diapers, smoothed the bed sheets, caressed him until he fell asleep then woke up again, struggling for air. Every four hours, Belzora would give him shots of morphine to soothe the pain.

The doctor came in one day and said that he didn't expect Duke to live through the week. His mother Doris whom I had called despite Duke forbidding me to, flew from Chicago. She came huffing and puffing, waving her finger in my face.

"What you done to my baby? What you done now to Duke? Where is he? I want to see . . ."

"I ain't taking you to the bedroom until you calm down," I told her.

"Duke's too sick and much too weak to put up with your jive."

"Who do you think you are, talking to me like that? I'm his mother. I have a right to . . ."

"No! You ain't moving from this living room," I said, blocking her way.

"Come on, you two," Belzora whispered from the bedroom door. "Quit that cat-dog fight right now!"

"Sis, stay out of this. It's between Doris and me," I said as I pushed my sister inside the bedroom and shut the door after her. "Woman, you and I got some serious business to iron out."

"You ain't got nothing to say to me that I want to hear," she shouted. "You've perverted my son. You are killing him, low-down immoral, son of the devil . . ."

"Don't you ever talk to me about morality. You have been blessed with four sons but as I understand, each one by a different father and you've never even been married."

"Shut your dirty mouth before you say things even God can't forgive you for," she yelled, lifting her hand as if to strike me.

"Don't you try it," I said, holding back her arms and putting my hands over her mouth to muffle her screams.

"Go ahead, bite me! You'll get blood in your mouth and who knows, I might be infected too. Go ahead! You'll see if this disease discriminates between gays and straights. Go right ahead! Take a big bite," I kept taunting her. She froze.

"Now, you're finally going to hear me out. Yes, you will," I told her, restraining her as she tried to move away. "I met you once, nine years ago Thanksgiving, when Duke and I went to Chicago, on our first trip together. You didn't like me then and you still don't like me. I didn't like you then and I still don't like you. But damn it, I was willing to give you a chance because you are Duke's mother and I respected that. You were so mean when he told you about our relationship. You ordered him to break up with me and move back to Chicago because New York City was corrupting him. He was sobs and tears on our flight back. I remember he couldn't wait to get to the dorm that Sunday night, to call you. He was shaking from all the mean things you were saying to him on the phone. How you didn't want to have anything more to do with him if he didn't repent. How you couldn't have such a sinner as a son. He was so broken, and it hurt me that you had hurt him so bad. I couldn't believe that a mother would actually be that cruel. Woman, he loved you but he loved me too. I remember that I took him in my arms, rocked him all night long. Right then and there, we promised each other that we were going to be together forever; hooked for life. So we both helped each other through graduation. I got involved with a record company and he became a damn good accountant. We rented this apartment and been living together ever since, man and man. Doris, I have been good to your son and Duke has been so good to me, in ways you can't begin to imagine. I don't expect you to like it and I don't care if you dislike it but this is our story, just the way it is . . ." It was then and only then that I released her from my grip.

"Can I see my baby now?" she whispered.

That Friday at 3:00 p.m.—while his mother sat on the bed, holding his left hand and reading the twenty-third psalm, and I sat on the bed, holding his right hand and reliving all our good memories—trusting the instant, Duke yielded his soul.

There were no tears. There was no time for tears that year. Just a tight knot in the pit of my chest where it hurts more each day. Yet, it had all come to this: a two-pound plastic bag filled with a promise gone, scattered dreams—can't even pick up the pieces—all too quick.

State of Siege

Nile is often startled out of deep sleep when someone steps on the grate, six stories below. A cat jumps out of a garbage can, kids crash beer bottles, even when the window rattles in the wind, he is so startled that he gasps for breath as if all air blew out of him. In a flash, he pulls out the nine-inch knife under his pillow—the nine-inch knife sharpened and soaked regularly in vinegar with red hot chili peppers, the nine-inch knife he hopes will come in handy—he sits on the bed, straight, still. He waits twenty minutes; an hour or two; many times until daybreak when he kisses the knife softly, puts it back under his pillow, rolls up his body like a ball, crawling into himself, alone with memories and the pain of that night—so long ago now—like many New York City August nights, treacherous.

No air conditioner and no fan, the heat made him twist in bed. He got up about midnight, pulled up the shades, opened wide the fire-escape window—the only window in the bedroom—even a breeze was a hard bargain to wish for but at least he could view the full moon; toast it with cheap white wine which can cool and make one feel good like nothing else does. Nile lay naked on sweat-drenched sheets; dreams beamed down.

He dreamt he was a catfish in the middle of the Mississippi River. Fresh water flowed over him, under him, all around him—everywhere water flowed—soft, soothing, clear, caressing him, and he was swimming away when suddenly he felt fingers hook his neck.

He panicked and tried to scream but the fingers were choking him. He kicked mad, pushed the attacker aside, knelt on the bed, looking for anything to whack the attacker's head with when he heard him growl: "If you make one more move, I'll can your fuckin' face."

The attacker hammered his foot into Nile's spine, pinning him down on the bed while he twisted his arms behind his back.

"Little faggot, I been watchin' you . . ."

"Don't you call me no faggot," Nile yelled back. "Man, I got a girlfriend."

"Stop lyin', bitch!"

"She's real pretty."

"Shut up!"

"Her name's . . ."

"I said shut up," the attacker shouted as he pushed Nile down even harder into the mattress. "Next thing you gonna tell me, she's knocked-up with your kid. Love to hear yourself lie, don't you?"

"But I swear it. I swear," Nile kept muttering.

"I know a faggot when I see one and I seen you lots of times, swishin' your faggot ass down the avenue. I been wantin' that piece for some-time now."

Nile couldn't move so he slightly turned his head to look at the attacker. All he saw was a big body. Wide wild eyes peered out of a dark ski mask. He smelled whiskey. That look frightened him most. Nile trembled.

"I told you don't move," the attacker yelled, back-handed him across the head. Smack.

Nile's jaw cracked. He coughed out two front teeth and kept moaning, "Take anything you want, just don't hurt me."

The attacker kept yelling, "Bitch, I told you be quiet." Smack.

"Please don't hurt me . . ."

"Shut up!" Smack.

"I got money. There's plenty . . ."

"Oh yeah . . ."

"Down there . . . you can have it all. Please don't hurt me," Nile kept pleading.

"Where is it?"

"There's lots in that last drawer."

"Which one?"

"Bottom one. You'll find money . . . thirty dollars. I got money. I got at least thirty to thirty-five . . ."

"Thirty-five bucks ain't worth shit," the attacker yelled as he pulled out the whole drawer from the chest and dropped it on the floor. Nile tried to get up.

"Don't you move one fuckin' inch," the attacker shouted and threat-ened to backhand Nile one more time. "Holy Mary, female panties!" The attacker laughed loud.

"Those are leotards. I'm a dancer."

"I knew it, I knew it, I knew you was a fuckin' fag," the attacker kept laughing, throwing Nile's leotards all over the place. A cherry-red one here, a purple one there, a bright-orange over here, a baby-blue over there; all colors of the rainbow in all directions.

"Where did you stash that dough?"

"Inside that drawer, I swear. That's where I keep all my money."

"You better not be lyin' through your broken teeth again. I can't find . . ."

"Down there . . ."

"Now I see it!" The attacker laughed, grabbed the bills and counted them out loud. "Twenty-eight bucks! Can't buy horse-shit dope with that kind of dough. You gonna pay." The attacker grabbed Nile by his hair.

"Stop it! Stop it," Nile pleaded. He felt as if every root would come out of his scalp. The attacker pushed him down and pulled him up, pushed him down and pulled him up, pushed him down and pulled him up, again, again and again. Nile almost fainted.

"Twenty-eight bucks, you gonna pay. Now, get up. I said get up, bitch."

Nile lay there, quiet. He could hardly move.

"Put this panty on. You gonna do a little dance number for me."

Somehow Nile managed to sit on the bed and pulled the leotard up his legs. He stood up and his knees caved him.

"Oh no," the attacker yelled as he grabbed Nile. "You ain't gonna pass out on me. You gonna dance real slow, real sexy, side to side, just like I seen them hula hawaiian gals do it on them t.v. commercials."

Well, Nile just moved as he was told.

"Real good! Doing real good, baby. That's right . . . side to side, real slow and easy . . . just like a real sissy faggot. Ha-ha-ha . . ."

The attacker kept laughing, clapping his hands to give Nile some rhythm. He just kept moving, dancing best as he could then stopped and said "I'll do anything . . . a blowjob, anything you want."

"Oh! You like to suck cocks, don't you?"

Nile just stared at him. He didn't know what to say.

"Answer me!"

Slowly Nile softly said, "Yes, I like . . ."

"Loud! I want to hear you real loud."

Nile shouted, "YES/SIR/I'D/LIKE/TO/SUCK/YOUR/BIG/BLACK/COCK!"

"Now you talkin'!"

Nile quickly knelt on the bed, unzipped the attacker's dirty jeans and pulled out his cock. Uncut, average size, no big thing. Nile played with it for a while, tickled those big hairy balls, pushed the head in and out, trying to get it hard. Tough. No luck but he lowered his face and opened his mouth. The attacker immediately jumped away.

"Oh no you won't! So you can bite me!"

Nile fell back. He didn't know what to do. His mouth was hurting him. "There's some wine left," he muttered.

"Where?"

"On the floor . . ."

The attacker grabbed the bottle, put it to his mouth and spit out all he drank in Nile's face. "Holy shit, you wanna poison me, don't you?"

"I didn't mean to . . ."

"Bitch, stop lyin'. Now you're really gettin' my juice flowin'. I'm gonna stick it to you good."

The attacker rolled Nile over on his stomach and ripped a big hole in the leotard. Nile started to shake uncontrollably. The attacker bit him hard on the ass. Nile screamed. The attacker grabbed the pillow, put it all over Nile's head, spread-eagled him, lunged and plunged. Muffled cries . . . stiffled sighs . . .

Hours later when he woke up—blood seeping out of his swollen eyes, blood seeping out of his broken nose, blood seeping out of his twisted lips—Nile tried to stand up but his knees buckled. He couldn't walk. He couldn't talk. He dragged himself slowly across the floor to the window, climbed on the sill and passed out again.

At Bellevue Hospital, someone told him some school-girl had seen his naked body hanging on the fire-escape, a wine bottle sticking out of his ass and had called the cops.

Ever since, every night, he checks the double locks on the door. He checks that the window is shut tight. He checks that the nine-inch knife is where it must be and Nile slips into this state of siege.

Essays

"Depending on how you see the times
We're wasting time or in a moving line."

—Deee-Lite

Haiti: A Memory Journey

Early Friday morning, February 7, 1986, drinking champagne and watching televised reports of Haitian President-for-Life Jean-Claude "Baby Doc" Duvalier fleeing for his life aboard a U.S. Air Force plane, I can't help but reminisce about my childhood experiences, and reflect on the current political and social situation, along with my expectations as a gay man who was born and grew up there.

Having seen, so many times during this AIDS crisis, Haitian doctors and community leaders deny the existence of homosexuality in Haiti; having heard constantly that the first afflicted male cases in Haiti were not homosexual, but alas, poor hustlers who were *used* by visiting homosexual American tourists who infected them and thus introduced the disease into the country; having felt outrage at the many excuses, lies, denials, and apologies—I am duty-bound to come out and speak up for the thousands of Haitians like me, gay and not hustlers, who, for one reason or another, struggle with silence and anonymity yet don't view ourselves as victims. Self-pity simply isn't part of my vocabulary. Haunted by the future, I'm desperate to bear witness and settle accounts. These are trying times. These are times of need.

For years now, Haiti has not been a home but a cause to me. Many of my passions are still there. Although I did my best to distance myself from the homophobic Haitian community in New York, to bury painful emotions in my accumulated memories of childhood, I was politically concerned and committed to the fight for change in my native land. It's not surprising that the three hardest yet most exhilarating decisions I have faced had to do with balancing my Haitian roots and gay lifestyle. The first was leaving Haiti to live in the United States. The second was going back to meet my father for the first time. The third, tearing up my application to become a U.S. citizen. Anytime one tries to take fragments of one's personal mythology and make them understandable to the whole world, one reaches back to the past. It must be dreamed again.

I was born on October 2, 1957, one week after François (Papa Doc) Duvalier was elected President. He had been a brilliant doctor and a writer of great verve from the *Griots* (*negritude*) movement. Until that time, the accepted images of beauty in Haiti, the images of "civilization," tended to be European. Fair skin and straight hair were better than dark and kinky. Duvalier was black pride. Unlike previous dictators who had ruled the country continuously since its independence from the French in 1804, Duvalier was not and did not surround himself with mulattoes, a mixed-race group which controlled the economy. Duvalier brought *vodun* to the forefront of our culture and, later in his reign, used it to tyrannize the people.

I grew up in Les Cayes, a sleepy port city of 20,000 in southwest Haiti, where nothing much happened. Straight A's, ran like a girl, cute powdered face, silky eyebrows—I was the kind of child folks saw and thought quick something didn't click. I knew very early on that I was "different" and I was often reminded of that fact by schoolmates. *"Massici"* (faggot), they'd tease me. That word to this day sends shivers down my spine, but, being the town's best-behaved child, a smile, a kind word were my winning numbers.

We—mother (a registered nurse anesthetist), grandfather (a lawyer who held, at one time or another, each of the town's top official posts, from mayor on down), and I—lived in a big, beautiful house facing the Cathedral. The Catholic Mass, especially High Mass on Sundays and holy days, with its colorful pageantry, trance-inducing liturgy, and theatrical ceremony, spellbound me. And that incense—that incense took me heaven-high each time. I was addicted and I attended Mass every day. Besides, I had other reasons. I had developed a mad crush on the parish priest, a handsome Belgian who sang like a bird.

I must have been seven when I realized my attraction to men. Right before first communion, confused and not making sense, I confessed to this priest. Whether he understood me or not, he gave me absolution and told me to say a dozen Hail Marys. Oh Lord, did I pray. Still, girls did nothing for me. Most of my classmates had girlfriends to whom they sent passionate love poems and sugar candies, and whom they took to movies on Sunday afternoons. All I wanted to do with girls was skip rope, put make-up on their faces, and comb their hair. I was peculiar.

Knowing that I probably would never marry, I decided that I wanted to be a priest when I grew up. For one, priests are celibate, and I had noticed that many were effeminate. Some even lisped, like me. I built a little altar in my bedroom with some saints' icons, plastic lilies, and colored candles and dressed in my mother's nursing uniform and petticoat. I said Mass every night. The Archbishop of Haiti, François W. Ligondé, a childhood friend of my mother and uncles, even blessed my little church when he once visited my family. I was so proud. Everybody felt that I'd be the perfect priest, except my mother, who I later found out wanted me to become a doctor like my father—who I never met, never saw pictures of, never heard mention of, and accepted as a nonentity in my life.

I used to believe that I was born by Immaculate Conception, until one day I was ridiculed in school by my science teacher, who had asked me for my father's name. When I told him of my belief, he laughed and got the entire class to laugh along. Until then, I had never questioned the fact that my last name was the same as that of my mother, who was not married. It was then that I smelled foul play and suspected that I was the result of sexual relations between my mother and grandfather. I didn't dare ask.

In the early 1960s, Papa Doc declared himself President-for-Life and things got worse and worse. I remember hearing of anti-Duvalier suspects being arrested. I remember hearing of families being rounded up and even babies being killed. I remember the mysterious disappearances at night, the mutilated corpses being found by roads and rivers the next day. I remember the public slayings, adults whispering and sending my cousins and me to another room so they could talk. Rumors of invasions by exiled Haitians abounded. Some of these invasions were quickly stopped by government forces. The *tontons macoute* (bogeymen) were everywhere, with their rifles slung over their shoulders and their eyes of madness and cruelty.

Poverty was all around me and, in my child's mind, I had accepted this. Some had, some had not. Fate. Cyclones, hurricanes, floods came and went. Carnival was always a happy time, though. Dressed in a costume, I, along with thousands took to the streets each year with our favorite music bands. Grandmother died during Mardi Gras '65.

I was miserable for weeks and kept a daily journal to her. Soon after, mother left for Switzerland and I moved in with my aunt Marcelle and her husband.

In 1968, my aunt had her first and only child. Was I jealous! I had been quite comfortable and so spoiled for three years that when she gave birth to Alin, it was difficult for me to accept that I was not her real child, a fact I'd at times forgotten. That year she gave me a beautiful birthday party. My schoolmates were making fun of me more than ever. I still wanted to be a priest. I said a Mass for Martin Luther King, Jr., and Bobby Kennedy when each was assassinated. Duvalier declared himself the flag of the nation and became more ruthless. I took long walks on the beach by myself. It was a year of discovery.

One afternoon, I saw Pierre swimming alone. He called me to join him. I was surprised. Although we went to the same school and we had spoken to each other once or twice, we were not buddies. Three or four years older, tall and muscular, Pierre was a member of the volleyball team and must have had two or three girlfriends. I didn't have a swimsuit, so I swam naked. I remember the uneasiness each time our eyes met, the tension between us, my hard-on. We kept smelling each other out. He grabbed me by the waist. I felt his hard dick pressing against my belly. Taut smiles. I held it in my hand and it quivered. I had never touched another boy's dick before. I asked him if he had done this with other boys. He said only with girls. Waves.

He turned me around and pushed his dick in my ass. Shock. I remember the pain. Hours later, the elation I felt, knowing that another person who was like me existed. In Les Cayes, there had been rumors about three or four men who supposedly were homosexual, but they all were married. Some had no less than seven children. Knowing Pierre was a turning point for me. The loneliness of thinking that I was the only one with homosexual tendencies subsided.

In 1969, man walked on the moon. I was happy. Pierre and I met each other three or four times (once in my grandfather's study, and he almost caught us). I didn't say anything about this to anyone, not even in confession. I didn't pray as much. I passed my *certificat*, which is like graduating from Junior High school in the U.S. Mother moved from Geneva to New York City, where I visited her in the summer of 1970.

To me, New York was the Empire State Building, the Statue of Liberty, hot dogs and hamburgers, white people everywhere, museums, rock music, 24-hour television, stores, stores, stores, and subways.

I remember the day I decided to stay in the U.S. A week before I was to go back to Haiti, my mother and I were taking a trip to Coney Island. Two effeminate guys in outrageous short shorts and high heels walked onto the train and sat in front of us. Noticing that I kept looking at them, my mother said to me that this was the way it was here. People could say and do whatever they wanted; a few weeks earlier thousands of homosexuals had marched for their rights.

Thousands! I was stunned. I kept thinking what it would be like to meet some of them. I kept fantasizing that there was a homosexual world out there I knew nothing of. I remember looking up in amazement as we walked beneath the elevated train, then telling mother I didn't want to go back to Haiti. She warned me of snow, muggers, homesickness, racism, alien card, and that I would have to learn to speak English. She warned me that our lives wouldn't be a vacation. She would have to go back to work as a night nurse in a week, and I'd have to assume many responsibilities. After all, she was a single mother.

That week I asked her about my father and found out that they had been engaged for four years while she was in nursing school and he in medical school. She got pregnant and he wanted her to abort. A baby would have been a burden so early in their careers, especially since they planned to move to New York after they got married. Mother wouldn't abort. She couldn't. Though the two families tried to avoid a scandal and patch things up, accusations were made, and feelings hurt. Each one's decision final, they became enemies for life.

Why Winnie Mandela Should Go to Jail

"The native is an oppressed person whose
permanent dream is to become the persecutor."
—Frantz Fanon, *The Wretched of the Earth*

Homophobia reared its ugly head before, during, and after the Winnie Nonzamo Mandela trial in Johannesburg. Along with three co-defendants, she stood accused of four counts of kidnapping and four more counts of assault to commit grievous bodily harm against the popular 14-year-old anti-apartheid activist James (Stompie) Moeketsi Seipei and three other young men, Gabriel Mekgwe, Kenneth Kgase, and Thabiso Barend Mono.

These youths were forcibly removed on December 29, 1988, from a Methodist manse in Soweto where they were living. Their abduction was an attempt to make them confess that they were police informers, but more importantly to rescue them from alleged sexual abuse by the white minister in charge of the manse, Rev. Paul Verryn, whose homosexual lifestyle they were supposedly embracing.

The kidnappings were allegedly carried out under Mrs. Mandela's orders by members of the Mandela United Football Club. They acted as her bodyguards while African National Congress (ANC) leader Nelson Mandela was still serving a state-imposed internment for life.

Allegedly led by Mommy (the name with which her bodyguards refer to Mrs. Mandela), these beatings happened in her home where she judged those abducted young men as "not fit to be alive." Seipei's dead body was discovered on January 6, 1989, with multiple stab wounds to the neck.

For two years, the South African government attempted to avoid bringing Mrs. Mandela to trial, although ample evidence and eyewitness accounts linked her to these crimes. It sought to avoid at all costs fueling the anger of the anti-apartheid movement, whose influence had grown tremendously during the last decade—enough to secure the international sanctions which have overwhelmed the South African economy.

Furthermore, bringing Mrs. Mandela to trial could be seen as a cheap, divisive ploy to harass the ANC and humiliate Nelson Mandela who—with millions watching live via satellite, including myself—after twenty-seven years of solitary confinement, on a clear bright Sunday, February 11, 1990, hand in hand with his wife, finally emerged from the Victor Verster Prison. His freedom became the most powerful symbol of apartheid resistance and human endurance, and the key to South Africa's democratic destiny.

Nevertheless, Winnie Mandela's trial got underway. I followed its proceedings with avid interest because of my concern for the welfare of Mrs. Mandela and the future of the anti-apartheid movement, but also because I am an HIV-positive gay black poet who keeps tabs on incidents of racism and homo-AIDS phobias wherever they take place, especially in so-called progressive gay or black circles.

As the trial started, I was appalled by Mrs. Mandela's lies, half-truths, and contradictions during her evasive court testimony. I was also appalled by some of her supporters' threats of reprisal against those who might testify against her. I was horrified by the mysterious disappearances, kidnappings, and possible murders of some prosecution witnesses.

I was appalled by her defense team's strategy of discrediting those who still dared to take the witness stand against her with allegations of homosexuality. (After all, in this country, haven't we seen lawyers use the "homosexual panic argument" to get gay-bashers and killers a lesser sentence or an acquittal?) I was appalled when I saw network newscasts of Mrs. Mandela's supporters parading outside the courthouse with anti-gay posters and placards.

I recall one night watching a telecast of Mrs. Mandela vehemently denying the existence of homosexuality in indigenous black culture. That was news to me, because I was born, raised, and I came out in Haiti—the most African-rooted of all nations in the Western Hemisphere. I have also vacationed in the Caribbean and Africa, where I have met several black homosexuals who have never ventured outside their homelands. I'm also well aware of the nonjudgmental acceptance of homosexuality in many African tribal cultures such as the Lango, the Konso, the Cilenge-Humbi, the Ovimbundu, the Kimbundu, the Barea-Kunama, the Manghabei, the Ambo, the Bantu, the Kwanyama, the

Korongo, the Masakin, and especially the West-African Yoruba religion which thrives in the Americas. In Haitian *vondun*—a derivative of the Yoruba religion—priestesses are called *mambo*: a term synonymous with lesbians.

Come to think of it, I now recall seeing on television a prior incident when the South African police were roughing up Mrs. Mandela's grandchildren. She shouted: "Don't touch my kids! You might have AIDS!" I had certainly expected better of Mrs. Mandela, but back then, I could excuse those comments as unfortunate and expressed at a time of great duress. I had also simply come to accept her pattern of homophobia and "AIDS" panic as two more examples of common behavior on the part of many leaders in our international black community, which from day one has been disproportionately affected by the epidemic—a fact which has been covered up and for which we—especially some African countries and Haiti—will pay dearly for years to come. (For the record, the ANC has included a clause forbidding discrimination on the basis of sexual orientation in the bill of rights which it has formulated. Nelson Mandela himself has commented favorably on lesbian and gay civil rights. Perhaps he had witnessed gay behavior first-hand while he was incarcerated. He might have learned a thing or two about that which most Africans still hypocritically claim is a white man's import).

However, the cold tone in which Mrs. Mandela had spoken left a sour taste in my mouth, as much as candidiasis, and as much as what I had perceived to be her casual endorsement of the "necklace" form of coercion.

Throughout the trial, I kept reflecting on what Mrs. Mandela has meant to me over the years. I remember my awe as I watched her time after time on television. In colorful native clothes, there she was stomping the ground with supporters while they chanted freedom songs. First in the air, there she was standing by the ANC colors-draped coffin of a fallen comrade. Her face drained, there she was leaving the jail after one of her weekly visits to Mr. Mandela. There, here, everywhere, hers was always a dedicated spirit and indomitable strength.

No matter how much she suffered from the alienation, the exile, the tribulations, and the "trials" of apartheid, she suffered, she sacrificed and single-handedly managed to raise her kids, hold on to her sanity, and safeguard their lives. Under pressure herself, she led us to keep the pressure on the South African government. Unfortunately, she also led some of her supporters to apply physical pressure (better known as torture) on some of her dissenters in the freedom movement.

On May 13, 1991, after Justice N.S. Stegmann (who presided over the trial; there are no jury trials in South Africa) found Mrs. Mandela guilty of "bearing a heavy responsibility" in those crimes, I remember watching her on television walk out of the courthouse, waving her arm, broad smile and all, vowing to appeal and win, as if her conviction had been a total fabrication and misrepresentation of justice. But I also recall seeing a somewhat shaken and somber Nelson Mandela by her side, holding her other arm. That frame of contrasting figures is etched in my memory.

Bold headlines, angry editorials, fierce columns in African-American newspapers and magazines were swift in denouncing Mrs. Mandela's conviction for being an accessory to those assault charges. The sentence itself carried a maximum of six years in jail.

Ad Hoc Committees and press conferences, letter-writing and telephone campaigns, demonstrations and rallies were organized to generate international support. "A Day of Absence" for black women in New York City was proposed for June 4 in protest.

Official statements poured in from such well-known African-American national leaders as Jesse Jackson, Coretta Scott King, and New York City Mayor David Dinkins. They sang in a chorus of protest to demand that Mrs. Mandela not be imprisoned.

Some supporters in America and abroad declared that in a racist South African court system which upholds apartheid laws, Mrs. Mandela could never have gotten a fair trial. Others saw the trial as a cover-up for a larger government agenda as despicable and treacherous as that agenda's well-known financial and military support of vigilantes and hit-squads from the Inkhata organization. The chief of the Inkhata, Gatsha Buthelezi, is steadfast in his opposition to Nelson Mandela, to sanctions, and to the armed struggle of the ANC, with which his Zulu followers daily engage in a bloody conflict that continues to claim thousands of lives. Some reiterated that the conviction was one more desperate government-devised plot to delay apartheid's demise. Others insisted that it was a tactic to break the spirit of the freedom movement and weaken the ANC, especially Nelson Mandela's position regarding negotiations.

Nowhere in Mrs. Mandela's supporters' denouncements did I ever hear anybody question whether justice for young Seipei's torture, then subsequent murder, was rendered. Nowhere did I hear loud and clear denouncements of Mrs. Mandela's lawyers' homophobic antics from any of our African-American national leaders, many of whom are allegedly pro-lesbian and gay rights and have greatly benefited from lesbian and gay community support.

In the aftermath of the trial of Mrs. Mandela, I have also pondered the implications regarding the inclusion of lesbian and gay rights in the broader struggle for a democratic, unitary South Africa. Not one given to being cynical because I acknowledge the power of hope, I still live with too many questions.

Should Winnie Mandela not go to jail because she is Nelson Mandela's wife? Should Winnie Mandela not go to jail because she was separated from her husband for twenty-seven years, therefore the couple should be spared another forced separation? Should Winnie Mandela not go to jail because as she claims, she was subjected to a public trial in the white-controlled international news media, long before her actual court case started? Should Winnie Mandela not go to jail because South African whites have never been brought to trial *en masse* for the century of innumerable inhumane crimes they have committed—and continue to perpetrate—against South African Blacks? Should Winnie Mandela not go to jail because all black people imprisoned in South Africa are *de facto* political prisoners? Should Winnie Mandela not go to jail because South African Blacks might get more angry, sparking more violence and bloodshed? Should Winnie Mandela not go to jail because she's the "Mother of the Nation"? Should Winnie Mandela not go to jail because a gay youth was murdered—good riddance and so what?

On the television program *Like It Is*, Gil Noble asked Karen Daughtry, wife of activist Reverend Herbert Daughtry of Brooklyn, to review the events that led to the kidnapping and assault charges against Mrs. Mandela. "In plain simple English, were these rundown conditions that this youngster was living in?" he asked. She replied: "I have heard that there have been some charges of homosexuality and some kind of behavior on the part of the adult that had these young men . . ." To which Gil Noble could only sigh: "Oh . . . oh . . . ." Wrong time for an investigative reporter to be so dumbfounded; one could scarcely assume that he was in fact moaning over one more instance of our African-American community's homophobia.

The *Amsterdam News* reported that Mrs. Daughtry, who now is one of the leaders of an Ad Hoc Committee To Free Winnie Mandela, declared before she was arrested for blocking the entrance of the South African consulate in Manhattan: "Winnie Mandela symbolizes African women globally—past, present and future—our pain, our strength, our commitment and our audacity." That last word was a curious choice, because the dictionary defines it as "contemptuous of law." Audacity is, however, a vital necessity for any black person living in South Africa.

We African-Americans tend to cherish a romantic view of Africa as utopia. We often have a blurred vision of a continent where a culture of oppression, corruption, hunger, famine, and disease are as pervasive as our collective ignorance, denial, and rewriting of its history. Only after my travels through Africa some years ago did I realize that slavery was not a European invention; I also came to revise many other concepts I had grown up believing.

Too often, black nation after black nation has been freed from the cruelties of colonialism only to be taken over by some of the cruelest dictators known to mankind. The tragic case of my mother-country Haiti is only one sorry example. Freed from Napoleon's ruthless dominion by a slave rebellion in 1804, Haiti became the first black republic in the world, and the second republic in the New World after the United States. Yet after 187 years of independence and dictatorships, only this year did it finally get its first democratically-installed government. Better late than never, and may Father Aristide's election prove to be a trend. Still . . . .

Out of forty-five black nations on the continent of Africa, I can count on one hand the number of those with examples of freely elected governments. The rest are either military dictatorships whose leaders give themselves unlimited tenures through gross abuse of power, civil liberties, and public funds, or these nations are one-party states, democratic in name only, despotic in reality, true to tradition. After all, aren't these heads of state simply twentieth-century replicas of tribal chiefs?

In the last three decades only Leopold Senghor of Senegal, Julius Nyere of Tanzania, and Alhmed Ahidjo of Cameroon have voluntarily stepped down as heads of state. And in fact, each one of those had held office for at least twenty years.

While we must denounce the horrors of apartheid, we should be every bit as vehement in our denunciation of black totalitarianism on the African continent. As vehemently as we protest the murders committed by whites against blacks, we must vehemently protest the murders of blacks by blacks on the African continent, but especially in America, where the statistics of such crimes reflect genocidal proportions.

It has recently become apparent to me that as African-Americans, we are obsessed with whiteness. Our blackness is always relative to whiteness. We display much more public hurt and anger when *they* attack *us*. The black community's reaction to young Yussef Hawkins's vicious slaying in Bensonhurst by a group of racist white teenagers—and its aftermath—is a case in point.

Demonstrations were organized—rightfully so—by Al Sharpton and activist attorneys Mason and Maddox, whose loud voices are necessary to our African-American community (in fact to the country), and could be much more powerful and effective if they focused on empowerment rather than on blame and divisiveness. They decried the slaying and all the racist bias that went along with it. Indeed, for an African-American to be "lynched" by a mob of whites signifies how far we have advanced in American society.

But around the same time of Yussef's murder in Brooklyn, young Donald White—his mother's only child, a brilliant student and role model in his Queens neighborhood—met a dissimilar but as brutal a fate while he was going to do his mother's laundry. That Sunday morning in October, the laundromat wasn't open yet when he arrived at 6:00 a.m. While he waited outside for the doors to open, he was robbed of two dollar bills and $10 worth of quarters, then shot to death by another African-American teenager.

I don't recall any outrage regarding Donald White's murder. Do you? I have never seen his name emblazoned on a T-shirt. Have you? How many of us have buried in our consciousness all the other lives like Donald White's that too often are felled when they are too young, too gifted, and too black? Who mourns? Who remembers? Who marches?

Tell me: what's the difference between a black person attacked by a white person and a black person attacked by another black person? Hate? Self-hate? Perhaps we should quickly review our history.

First of all, when a white person is attacked by another white person we all hear about it. White people control the media and all the news they make as a people is a major part of "all the news that's fit to print or broadcast." When a white person is attacked by a black person, that too becomes news, because the white media gladly shows us one more example of black "bestiality." The Central Park jogger rape case is a fine example.

When a black person is attacked by a white person, we all hear about it, greatly due to black protests. Michael Griffith's murder is a fine example. So is the more recent baseball bat beating of Alfred Jermaine Ewell in Atlantic Beach, Long Island. But very few people read more than a blurb when a black person is viciously attacked by another black person. That latter category of assault outdistances all the others by many thousands of instances every year in our country, but it remains unimportant to the white media. Whites are not primarily affected by that form of crime.

According to statistics, and due to the high incidence of murders, an African-American male child born in Harlem, New York, has less of a chance of surviving to age fifty than a male child born in the poorest country on this earth, Bangladesh.

One quarter of young African males are either in jail, just coming out of jail, on bail, on parole, or on their way right now to jail. I am tired of hearing that ironical excuse that they/we are victims. Most of them/us are guilty of crimes primarily against each other/ourselves and for which they/we wish to bear no responsibility.

The kidnappings and assault charges for which Mrs. Mandela was convicted bear a similarity in their destructiveness and must not go unpunished. Oppression is oppression is oppression, no matter what form it takes, and it must be fought at all costs, on all levels. I am fully aware that my conception of the trial has been colored by its depiction in the white media, but not my perception. As Justice Stegmann stated when he imposed his sentence on Mrs. Mandela: "She fundamentally misunderstood her responsibilities when she conspired to deprive the four victims of their liberty."

Mrs. Mandela is Winnie Nonzamo Mandela. Winnie Nonzamo Mandela is not Nelson Mandela. Nelson Mandela is not the ANC. The ANC is not the monolithic voice of the South African freedom movement, which should bear no guilt-by-association in all this mess. There is still so much work to be done.

I salute wholeheartedly the continuing South African struggle for freedom and eventual democracy. With the latter comes a first-and-foremost responsibility: To respect the inalienable rights of others, white and black, old and young, straight and gay. That respect must include the right of freedom of speech, for which Nelson Mandela was prepared to die without ever surrendering.

When we walk away from that fundamental principle, we are left stranded as usual with deferred dreams in the desert of our nightmares. While the old white albatross of racist history loses its grip but still looms large over its neocolonialist progeny, the young black albatross of our history's brutal dictatorships preys and multiplies. Both are irreverent about the sanctity of black life.

When will we finally notice that the red carpet we are rolling out for ourselves is only our dirty laundry, soiled mostly by our own hands with our own black blood? On our way "home" to the top, how are we to get through the mountains of our brothers and sisters' corpses blocking our horizon?

Preface to "The Road Before Us"

The Road Before Us could have taken a far different path. As its editor and co-publisher, what I wanted foremost was a collection that would provide one more stepping-stone on the road to gay black poetical empowerment. Too often this has been the road not taken.

Each poet in this volume is represented by one poem. Many faces, facets, and phases of our lives are painted in these selections. From the ancient African tribal shamanistic tradition, as in Craig A. Reynolds "The Moon singers," to the common contemporary father/son alienation, as in "Bermuda" by Jim Murell—we explore, we examine, we experience.

Some poems, such as Thomas Glave's glorious "Landscape in black," and Arthur Wilson's gut-wrenching, lay-it-all-out "One rawdog night when too much of my queer was showing," are epic in stature. Others, such as Rickey Butler's poignant "After the fuck" and Richard Witherspoon's delicious "Haiku," offer the precise minimum of words and images needed to make their effect.

Carl Cook's tender "Love letter #25" and Bil Wright's evocative "Miracle" are sensual paeans to defiant sex and love in the era of AIDS. Blackberri's sweet "Love song" and André De Shields' wicked "His(blues) story" are lyrics. Three contributions are short prose pieces that read well poetically.

I relish this mixture of styles, which are wide-ranging as our concerns. The myths, metaphors, and mundaneness of our gay black community, like those of any other community, broaden and deepen everyone's knowledge of what it is to be human.

Among the poets included, Melvin Dixon and Essex Hemphill's writings are of paramount importance. The images they weave with their pens are extraordinary and would stand out in any company at any time. It is almost impossible for any openly gay poet to get his work published, and a number of the poets here, have followed Hemphill's example and put out their own collections. However, most of the poets in this anthology have never appeared in a book before.

Check out Robert Westley's brutally honest "What's happening." Read aloud Marvin K. White's fiercely humorous "Last rights." How about Metaphora's glorious homage to the gender-bending vogue culture in "Poem for the club kids?" It is my dream that all these fine young writers will keep penning poetry, polishing their craft, and juicing up a literally dying art.

*   *   *

The title *The Road Before Us* is borrowed from a line in the poem "Hejira" that the late Redvers JeanMarie wrote about our friendship. He dedicated it to me. I cherish it. It is anthologized here. The choice of "gay black poets" rather than "black gay poets" was a personal one. I originally used the working subtitle *Gay African-American Poets*—to which some contributors strongly objected because they were not born in the United States and moreover have not chosen to naturalize as American citizens, as I have.

Afrocentrists in our community have chosen the term "black gay" to identify themselves. As they insist, black comes first. Interracialists in our community have chosen the term "gay black" to identify themselves. As they insist, gay comes first. Both groups' self-descriptions are ironically erroneous. It's not which word comes first that matters, but rather the grammatical context in which those words are used—either as an adjective or as a noun. An adjective is a modifier of a noun. The former is dependent upon the latter.

I have never labeled myself either Afrocentrist or interracialist. From reading or seeing my theater pieces, many might characterize me as an Afrocentrist; but others might immediately characterize me as a n interracialist because I have loved and lived with a white man for the past eleven years.

Although I make no excuses or apologies for the racially bold statements in my writings, I also owe no one any justification of my "till-death-do-us-part" interracial relationship. While the *black gay* vs. *gay black* debate rages on, in much-needed constructive dialogue, we'd best ponder, as L. Lloyd Jordan did at the conclusion of his essay "Black Gay vs. Gay Black" (*BLK*, June 1990), "Who are gay blacks and black gays? Halves of a whole. Brothers."

Furthermore I consider my sexuality a preference. Most of us have an inclination to bisexuality that we don't acknowledge or act upon. I am very proud of my gayness, which is not to be confused with homosexuality.

In the preface to his book *Gay Spirit*, Mark Thompson explains this distinction clearly: "Gay implies a social identity and consciousness actively chosen, while homosexual refers to a specific form of sexuality. A person may be homosexual, but that does not necessarily imply that he or she would be gay." I declare that a person may be gay, but not necessarily homosexual.

Color (and it is so much more than skin pigmentation) is not a preference. The same has not to this day been scientifically demonstrated regarding our gayness, which is so much more than sexual orientation. It's hard to imagine that any writer in this anthology would ever want to change either his color or his gayness, given a choice.

I realize that these views add fuel to the "fire and brimstone" pronouncements of those in far-right politics who argue that we lesbians and gays could change to "normal" if we wanted to.

While I agree with our lesbian and gay community's tenet that some of us can't change, I would stand up anytime to Jesse Helms and his ilk, and declare loudly that, whatever the case may be, *I refuse* to change. Far too many of us continuously let church and state dictate our fate, by submitting to their painful spiritual and political butt-fuck.

What does all this politics have to do with poetry? As Judy Grahn said in a keynote address at OutWrite '90, "Poetry predicts us, tells us where we are going next."

Shouldn't we, the poets in this anthology, dispatch to Helms our gay black poems each time he gets up in front of the Senate and spews forth yet another homophobic or racist harangue without fairness of debate and real challenge? Couldn't fifty of us (one representing each state of siege that he wants to turn our USA into) also fax him full-size etchings of our dicks to be inserted in *The Congressional Record*. Then ours would not be the dicks of death as popularly characterized, but truly the dicks of everlasting political life.

*   *   *

Some months ago, I urged all the contributors who are HIV-positive or have AIDS to come out. I felt then, and I still feel, that there is nothing that those of us in this predicament could reveal in our bios that is more urgent and deserving of mention than our seropositivity or diagnosis.

A number of contributors agreed. I applaud their trust and thrust. Others who have previously come out publicly chose not to do so in this instance. A few whom I know to be in the last stages of HIV illness cited confidentiality, and their right of privacy.

While sympathetic to the right of privacy issue, I also find it part of the overall problem. It fosters anonymity rather than visibility. And when we don't show en masse the lives, the faces, and the hearts of AIDS—ours included—we are accepting all the connotations of shame, all the mystification of sin and repentance that those who are plainly simple-minded place on a virus.

AIDS is a Pandora's box. There is real jeopardy in revealing seropositivity, publicly or privately. In gay black poetry, the issue has been primarily dealt with from a third-person narrative rather than a first-person focus.

Meanwhile, in highly disproportionate numbers compared to our percentage in the American population, and adding to the lowering of our expected paltry sixty-year-or-so life span as black men, there are many gay disappearing acts among us, too often played solo, or for a small—and not so captive—audience. As the late Joseph Beam, editor of *In the Life*, anticipated and stated: "These days the nights are cold-blooded and the silence echoes with complicity."

So far no one has given me a valid explanation for Beam's silence regarding his illness. (For those who may not know, his body was discovered in an advanced stage of decomposition.) What kind of indictment of his preaching on behalf of the gay black community is that, for him not to have reached out to us? What kind of indictment is that of us, especially those who were privy to his AIDS diagnosis, for not having fully reached out to him?

Back in April 1988, Joe stayed overnight at my apartment as he always did when he visited New York City. I detected the syndrome beneath the moodiness, innuendoes, and fungus of the fingers. I did not disclose to him my own seropositivity, although thinking of it now, I believe that he detected more than just holocaust obsession in the poems I shared with him.

What kind of "deadly guessing" game were Joe and I, two of the better-known gay black writers, supposedly leaders, and most importantly friends, playing with each other? What kind of label do I attach to my name, after leaving unreturned messages on his answering machine, for not marching down to Philadelphia and knocking on/down his door?

Yes, I am sick of the destructive threats that HIV constantly poses to my life-partner, my lovers, my friends, my communities, and me. On my desk, pictures of Redvers, David, and Ortez, to whose memory this anthology is dedicated, are framed like icons.

Each time I write, I hear their voices, backed by a chorus of others I loved ("One AIDS death every eight minutes; it ain't enough to write; you gotta demonstrate") pound in my head, like those sanctifying drums, especially *tambou assôto*, I used to hear, in my childhood, in Haiti, in the hours of darkness.

*   *   *

May the rhythm of our gay black hearts be as uplifting in our daily lives as it is in our essays, anthologies, films, rallies, one-night-stands, and poems.

May the rhetoric never rage like the grandstand of many pedantics in the gay white community, which we so often hasten to castigate for claiming to speak on behalf of our "rainbow" community.

And most of all, may we come to believe in each other—heroes, first, to ourselves— unafraid to "strike a pose" and take a stand.

Ours is a country where omens abound out of control. Ours is a country tempted by fascism. Ours is a country in a demythologized age, perhaps void of salvation. Yet I don't believe in the destruction of America, but in a reconstitution that recognizes our fully participating gay black voices. Silence = Death. Writing = Life. Publishing = Survival.

With sixty T-cells left, I live on borrowed time. However, self-pity and sympathy are not part of my survival kit—another factor why making this book a reality became a first priority.

But when I do die, killed like hundreds of thousands in this AIDS war, may it transpire that every Memorial Day—until the circus of media, clown masks of stigma, and jeers of hysteria stop in our country; and certainly until a cure is found, or at least until a do-or-die governmental, scientific and societal commitment to discover one finally gets underway—my life-partner, mother, lovers, friends, fellow poets, somebody, anybody . . . burn the Stars and Stripes, then toss the ashes over my grave.

And please don't sing "The Star-Spangled Banner"—but, furiously, read back every poem in the following pages.

Assoto Saint, *nom de guerre*
Summer 1991
New York City

A Match With Ashe

"A gay activist wrote that I had a moral obligation to go public with my condition. That's bullshit."
—Arthur Ashe, WCBS-TV

The conspiracy of silence regarding AIDS bestowed upon former tennis great Arthur Ashe by various reporters four years prior to his April 8 press conference was generous but erroneous. It was part of the regretful mystification of HIV and the shameful vilification of people with AIDS as bearing a condition about which they should be aided to keep tight-lipped under the guise of our constitutional right of privacy.

Ashe was driven to a point of no return by *USA Today* sports reporter Doug Smith and sports editor Gene Policinski's phone calls to confirm a tip about his HIV illness. Cornering him made a solid point for outing celebrities not only on account of queerness but also as to their AIDS diagnosis. Indeed, the public had a legitimate right to know—especially when one happens to be, like Ashe, a respected and beloved figure in the community of people of African descent. It is a community that is, in this country and internationally, disproportionately affected by this pandemic and that is among the most poorly served with health care, HIV education, and prevention. Yet it is a community that has—until recently—remained invisible and powerless in this crisis due to several factors, including denial, the refusal of people of color with HIV to come out and misfocused leadership. (While people of African descent make up 12% of the American population, we constitute 30% of all national reported AIDS cases.)

Just as Ashe's decade-long list of medical struggles was front-page news, with or without his permission, so should his HIV illness be. I don't recall Ashe manifesting any shame or fear of disclosure in 1979, when in the aftermath of his quadruple-bypass heart surgery, in his St. Luke's-Roosevelt Hospital pajamas, he displayed the disfiguring scar on his chest and stomach as he and cardiac surgeon John E. Hutchinson III explained the success of the operation. The media gathered en masse; tape machines recorded non-stop; cameras clicked away.

I can't help but wonder if Ashe would have eventually come out on his own, or if he would have continued to keep his HIV status hidden from the public until the end, much like other prominent African-Americans such as fashion designers Willi Smith and Patrick Kelly whose obituaries stated they died respectively of "pneumonia" and "bone marrow disease"; choreographer Alvin Ailey whose death was attributed to "dyscrasia" and Reverend James Cleveland who supposedly succumbed to "heart failure," to name but a few.

I do not doubt that if AIDS had struck those aforementioned on account of African genes, instead of homosexual intercourse with an infected partner, not only would they have publicly acknowledged their diagnosis, they would have initiated a full-fledged racial civil war to combat existing public apathy and lackadaisical commitment to finding a cure. They would have also worked tirelessly to gain sympathy as victims of racial prejudice.

Ashe was not challenged by the media about his unequivocal contention "that the cause of my HIV infection was a blood transfusion, either after my 1979 bypass operation or the 1983 operation." That statement, which could not be confirmed, either by Dr. Hutchinson or by his doctors at New York Hospital where he has been treated for AIDS, smacked of the divisiveness that exists in the HIV community between those puritanical illogicians labeled or who label themselves "innocent victims" and those of us who became infected through "deviant sexual behavior."

It is probable that Ashe, like almost 7,000 other Americans, became HIV-infected through blood transfusions before the antibody test was established in mid-1985. Since then, the national blood supply has been safeguarded through standard testing for HIV. All blood has been marked with donor numbers, which are used not only to identify patients who have been recipients of contaminated blood but also to notify donors who didn't know they were HIV-infected. However, I must add that, since mid-1985, the Centers for Disease Control have identified about 20 transfusion-associated cases. Contaminated blood may test seronegative because seropositivity is uncovered only after antibodies have formed, a period that can take anywhere from a few days to six months.

It is also probable—and of vital importance to speculate—that if Ashe had participated in just one incidence of unprotected sex, between 1978 and 1988 with somebody other than his wife Jeanne (who has tested negative), then he placed himself at risk for HIV infection. Basketball superstar Magic Johnson's announcement of his seropositivity last November, and his denial of homosexual encounters or IV-drug use, shocked the country into the realization that, in this health crisis, there are no high-risk groups. There are only high-risk behavior and tough luck.

"I knew even before Magic that if I wanted to go public I could possibly help," Ashe stated at his media-frenzied press conference. "But I wasn't ready to go public with it because I had some things that I wanted to do, unfettered, so to speak. I knew that with the public still learning about AIDS, that would have been impossible, once you go public."

How tragic that Ashe's refusal to voluntarily come forward until he was compelled to didn't further much-needed AIDS awareness during critical years. Compare this to Magic, who has, since his disclosure, managed to play in the National Basketball Association All-Star game and win the Most Valuable Player Award, co-written a book on AIDS and advocated for his right to participate in this summer's Olympics in Barcelona as a member of our national basketball team.

Ashe's April 28 statement at a Washington, DC, high school that "no AIDS activist and no AIDS activist group is going to force me to do anything I don't want to do," was disappointing and ungrateful. After all, didn't Ashe largely attribute his survival to his tolerance for AZT and aerosolized pentamidine, two drugs which AIDS activists, such as my late friend Ortez Alderson—even when he could barely walk and talk—fought the Food and Drug Administration and the National Institutes of Health to make available sooner than their red tape would have previously allowed. "Don't even try to pressure me into saying something or showing up at some event and thinking that somebody can shame me or embarrass me into doing it," Ashe arrogantly added.

Just as Ashe became the first African-American person named to the US Davis Cup team, the first—and only—African-American man to win the US Open, the Australian Open and Wimbledon, he missed an opportunity to doubly become the first black leading spokesperson on HIV and a living symbol of empowerment for people with HIV.

It is ironic that, throughout the first decade of the AIDS pandemic, Ashe has sat on the board of directors of Aetna Life and Casualty Co., where he helps to decide policy for one of our largest national insurance companies. At one time, Aetna barred gay men from coverage; to its discredit it continues to reject applications for new policies by people with AIDS or HIV. It is also ironic that Ashe is a longtime friend of President George Bush who called him on the morning of his AIDS announcement to wish him and his family well. Bush's health-care policies and politics of silence, like those of his predecessor Teflon Reagan, have, of course, contributed to this country's more than 160,000 AIDS deaths.

I am only too well aware of the overwhelming sense of despair that can numb anyone connected with this crisis. I have taken care of and buried, as a result of AIDS, five of the closest people to me. I have lost countless acquaintances to AIDS. I am surrounded by people with AIDS and HIV. My life-partner for the past 12 years is, like myself, a person with AIDS.

Contrary to the widely held belief, we are not all living with AIDS. Some of us are doing it on a much more personal level than others. It is our bodies, our minds, our spirits, that are disintegrating, little by little. On numerous occasions, I have lain on my apartment floor or in my bed, distancing myself from any responsibility, caught up in a surreal sense of time and place. On numerous occasions, I have walked past a building where one of my dead friends used to live, unable to continue walking. On numerous occasions, my memories have choked up my speech, my writings, my activism—making me question my survival, bringing me almost to the point of hopelessness. While I realize that neither Arthur Ashe nor Magic Johnson can cure AIDS, I do hope that, together, they will raise consciousness. But . . .

Will Ashe continue to sit on the board of Aetna, without challenging the insurance industry's prejudicial HIV policies? (So far, Ashe is the only national insurance company director who is publicly identified as a person with AIDS.) Will Ashe found or chair AIDS organizations and foundations to help alert inner-city youths to the risks of HIV, as he has started tennis clinics and founded or chaired many athletic organizations? Will Ashe appear in future forums on HIV policies, as he has appeared in numerous forums in connection with academic reform in intercollegiate athletics? Will Ashe add AIDS to his bibliography, as he has written prolifically on a variety of subjects ranging from academics, apartheid and athletics (including his three-volume masterpiece *A Hard Road to Glory: A History of the African-American Athlete*)? Will Ashe urge African-Americans with AIDS to use their diagnosis to promote civil rights, as he has urged African-American athletes to use their sports to advance civil rights?

Will Ashe exhort all the heads of our national African-American organizations to make the fight against AIDS part of their agenda, as he has continuously exhorted African-American leaders to make the fight against South African apartheid part of their agenda? (May they all challenge Louis Sullivan, the African-American secretary of health and human services, to stop his right-wing "house-niggah" dance while sidestepping major issues of this health crisis). Will Ashe be arrested as he protests the people-with-AIDS apartheid that closeted him for too long, as he was arrested at the South African Embassy while protesting apartheid? Will Ashe's myopic vision of this crisis clear up, and free him at last, now that the veil of hiding has been lifted?

Living with–dying of AIDS is not estimable in itself. However, fighting AIDS publicly is. I attach the label "person with AIDS" to my name, not as a badge of honor (although I am proud and unrepentant that I took part in the sexual revolution that raged in the '70s), but because we, the HIV community, especially those of us of African descent, must stand up and be counted. Not just as shadows inconspicuously dropping through horrific CDC statistics down into our graves, but as flesh-and-blood human beings, standing up for our constitutional rights to life.

ADDENDUM

In all the headlined tributes and glorious eulogies that appeared and were heard everywhere after Arthur Ashe's death on February 6, 1993, not one person so far has dared or cared to publicly reevaluate Ashe's forced disclosure of his AIDS condition. From that day, April 8, 1992, to this, the vast majority of people insist that Ashe's right of privacy around his HIV status was unnecessarily and brutally violated.

However, Ashe's eloquent speeches and his heroic actions on behalf of our HIV community during the months following his revelation serve as proof of the necessity to out celebrities with HIV.

Since his disclosure, Ashe enlisted the support of many of his tennis peers at the United States Open to participate in a 15-month, $5 million drive on behalf of the Arthur Ashe Foundation for the Defeat of AIDS. He also established the Arthur Ashe Institute for Urban Health, which is part of the State University of New York Health Science Center in Brooklyn.

Ashe was arrested while he took part in a demonstration against the Bush Administration's treatment of Haitian refugees, especially those who are qualified to enter the United States for political asylum, but are quarantined at Guantanamo Naval Base in Cuba due to their AIDS diagnosis or HIV-seropositivity.

Ashe spoke on the floor of the United Nations on World AIDS Day on December 1, 1992. As was reported in *The New York Times*, he considered that speech the most significant event in his life. The same paper also reported that he regarded the period since his disclosure the most productive period in his life.

While all this hoopla about the right of privacy continues, we must reaffirm, first and foremost, that our allegiance should be to the truth. The truth does not violate human beings but rather liberates them.

When a reporter asks a celebrity if s/he has AIDS and s/he denies it, if the reporter has evidence to the contrary, the reporter is under no obligation to participate in the cover-up. To do otherwise would be a miscarriage of the reporter's journalistic duties to seek the truth.

Simply put, Ashe's outing did more good for humanity and ultimately himself than if he had kept silent. Desperate times demand desperate actions.

I, too, will dearly miss Arthur Ashe.
February 14, 1993

Sacred Life: Art & AIDS

It is in our dreams that sacred life is entered. speak for our age. Escapism is a commitment to denial. Skepticism is healthy. Cynicism is a disease. Everybody's playing it. I offer myself hope, which is the very act by which man the unfulfilled in himself. Hope is not the kind of optimism that resolves all contradiction by blind leap into the future. Hope is engaged in the weaving of experience now in process, or in other words, in adventure now going forward. Despair is in a certain sense the consciousness of time as closed, or more exactly as still, of time as a prison, while hope appears to be piercing through time. Hope is greater than despair.

Movement that's happening through the world, whether it's in fighting apartheid, communism, dictatorships, sexism, homophobia, racism, AIDS phobia, and silence that's forced upon us, or most importantly that we force upon ourselves. Richard Wright once said that if you possess enough courage to speak out what you are, you will find out that you are not alone. Denies that white racism, straight homophobia ever had the power to reduce the black race to a traumatized martyrdom. Frying in the molten grease of defeat. Exhorts the gay and lesbian black community to fight crime, drugs, welfare dependency & teenage pregnancy, to shoulder responsibility, study diligently, debate reasonably & express its political will electorally. He should write not only what he understands, but open himself up to questions, and various possibilities. Face the movements of our time.

Theater narrows life down. Theater always presents itself in the present. On leaving the theater, the audience has to feel that it has awakened from stage dream/It narrows life down. it has explored some shared meaning, a catharsis. A writer should write not only what he understands, but also live with questions, always opening himself up to new ideas, possibilities, and rebirth, revolutionary terrorist committed supreme act of human courage, will & human power in killing indiscriminately, in the belief that there are no innocent people in a corrupt society. the artist recognized the criminal or revolutionary anarchist/terrorist as romantic, individual who set himself proudly and defiantly against, above, & beyond the laws & who embodied one of the possibilities of which artist and poet dreamed of, that of giving to the limits of his being regardless of the consequences. as men of color, we have always depended on spirits & music, depended on the elements to survive/I feel a rush/I will go on but: I will not forget you/nativist movement in america/By delving into our wants & needs, those things that make us tick, we discover that the essence of revolution and rebirth lies within. achieve his potential. Not only to survive but to grow tall and flourish. not to fight against but to fight for: eternal becoming. draw us out of ourselves into the community. translate raw emotion into imagery. Rejected the platonic supremacy of reason, embrace integrity of feelings. We must constantly stand firm against systems. a permanent indictment of the way this world closes in upon itself. Silence equals sin. Literature fails to act. Allowed to influence our destinies by the choices we make.

Latter prevents us from celebrating all the facets of our aliveness and declaring the truth. Our lives are a relentless unreality therefore we must create our own reality and invite our readers and audience to enter this reality. Lost souls trapped in the American dream. rapture of spirit. That's where true creation takes place. We must go to the limits of being regardless of the consequences. We must always remember this, and reassess our position as witness bearers, but also carriers of the torch of truth which often does scorch us. dungeons of low self esteem, archaic stereotypes, & self non-participation in the gay black struggle. cataclysmic night of upheaval that precedes purification and freshness. a writer who not only reflected the world, but tried to change it. cost of living lies, and price one pays for living those lies. Big game to be confused. everybody's playing it. man's why I publish. to break new ground, demolish barriers, to fight despite all odds. Don't just live in the here and now. nativist movement that America is losing its straight/bleak but sometimes memorable vision of a world out of control/ is in dreams that the pure sacred life is entered & direct relations with god, spirits, ancestral souls are re-established/voices, demonic & proud/ quest for holy ground/ point of departure is always an image/ the mystic hears the music within himself/ the unawakened man mere plays it/ experience the supernatural/

for the shaman does not simply make the journey we all dream making it/ he makes it on our behalf, as our envoy/ the shaman goes to the gods to present the wishes of the community/ his journey as inward & psychic/

man's nature, man's purpose in living, man's destiny, what is the good life/ a hysteric shows his own misery & desires by means of a symptom/ an artist submitting & being swept up my mystical forces heroes not totally understand/ he might be hallucinating or going insane/ we do not die in our dreams/ our will operates even in absurdity, even in the negation of possibility, even in the transmutation of lies from which truth can be remade/ unlike a musician or a painter, a writer needs a language. Obvious & not very interesting, until the question, which language/ our century is littered with examples of writers who have had to make a choice, to stick with, or abandon their mother tongue/ affirmation of a happy omen/ a hurricane of thoughts/ relationship between artist's private vision & audience understanding global village/ exploring common elements of human life without benefit of dogma/ creation rather than reaction/ soft touch moving into the anger/

turns precious & arty/ passion chills/ dedication wilts/ honesty deserts him, delighted in discoveries/ willing to take that feeling for human relations right through my writings/ I have access to the spirit world, to shadows, to animal understanding to guides & voices, visions, old ways of thinking, all the altered states of consciousness necessary for the core artistic creation/ the main purpose of ritual as it developed in tribal life is the creation of shared images/ awareness far distant from the human/ truth is beauty/something that lifts us above the everyday, meditate on the music/an artist being swept by mystical forces he does not totally understand/artistic freedom & adventure embodies the concept of liberation/ the song affirms mystical connection between primitive magic & modern technology, art & medicine, astrology & television, spiritual journey/ terror of aloness/ musical, spiritual, & political words transfigure one another/ fuck the masks, it's beyond the stage/unreasonable promises & requests/ but this ageless drama takes place in contemporary culture social, & political systems often countervail such fulfillment, whose spiritual institutions appear not to address the experience of living in the present age, & whose artistic milieu general shuns the expression of that aspiration/ our energies for the struggle ahead, idealist posture & utopian gesture/ a new feeling/ rebirth is basic spirit of revolutionary spirit/ cataclysmic night of upheaval that precedes purification & freshness of dawn/trying to get whole perspective of myself, & work with it/ a community celebrating & validating itself/ I will never allow incidents of racism to go by without fighting them/bigotry has to be fought no matter what form it takes/ warring elements within the self whose energies breed poetry on one hand, war on the other/ muse is not a quiet fire/free from responsibility & accountability/not only to survive but to grow & talk about it/ I'm the stand I take/ daily things taken for granted/ things that are anti-literary on the page, they seem quite literary on the stage/ the promise lives in the stand/ today, you begin to discover yourself, the mirror image/reflection which says go on/ a world of masks & disillusions/ another black queen done be digging up shit, talking loud, ain't stopping/ conviction, commitment & devotion/ fire raging in consciousness/activist & pacifist/ cannot cover the sun with both hands & say it's night/know what's about to be written will be written/ can't romanticize my inertia/interpret whole spectrum of human emotions/ I wish to create a work that will make a statement about my feelings and have somebody hear it/one night I am naked, I am stripped/ all my life, I have searched for something that pure/it's in my writings/possibility lives in our language and communication/loves being alive and worthwhile/responsibility: declaration that you are allowed to declare/our duty as human beings is to keep challenging ourselves individually and collectively/ part of that challenge is a willingness to learn, teach each other/ so you don't like me/ it's your problem/scared of me/somebody who's getting control of his feelings/the world is in desperate need of good challenge/you got to own it/the right to come out/glamorize my disease/ tears are necessary but they are not enough/ I sat there and thought to myself, if next year, I'm not here at this conference because I'm in my grave, or lying on a hospital bed, or in my own bed, too ill to travel, is that how as a PWA I would want to be remembered, by other people's tears/ on valentine's day, CMV while the day I left, the result of a lesion biopsy proved to be Kaposi's sarcoma/ the times when

I have failed, when younger authors have asked me to comment on their writings, when I have not taken the time to command and comment on their writings/it's such a necessary part of our development/ dialogue /so many of our leaders are poseurs/so many of our leaders and writers are just vogueurs/ will the muthafuckahs march up/past the anger, when a soft touch moves into the anger, and you are able to look back, reflect back on a crisis through writing about it/introspective perspective/yes, we have got to internalize this crisis, but there comes a time when we have got to externalize it also/ I have taken issue publicly with so many of our dead brothers, Joseph Beam, Craig G. Harris/ so strange/how can you review my work/ that year I won a fellowship in poetry from the New York State Foundation for the arts, and the James Baldwin award/vindication, not that I needed one since I know that I am a poet/

this is a country of immoral morals/ main ingredients: common sense and understanding/white house is one of the dirtiest places in the world/took me so long to move into myself/a vision of mythical consciousness/a voice demonic and proud/ investigate other gods and cultures/today you begin the task of writing life as it is happening/ everything is a thought first, triggered by some action somewhere, then registered on paper/each moment, age, brings its own predicament/laugh in the face of life/what effect has finding out meant to me/constant state of paranoia/destroyed by a fantasy forced upon him/good writing doesn't have to be sacrifice of another/release his energies and his power/ strip language to its root/freedom is discovery of limitations/black gay life is a relentless unreality/ engaged and empowered/touch us and penetrate to the core of language/like Latoya Jackson, sister is talking shit/man as a whole who's at issue/a quiet resolute sense of purpose/unite motion and emotion/poetry is what defines the self/

provide a god for the unbeliever/work with me instead of against me/as if my main purpose on this earth is to constantly seek people's love at all costs, to be liked/ I'm here to be respected and treated the same way you wish to be treated/ my duty is to tell the truth as I see it/ to elucidate and validate the human condition/

somebody who's coming to terms with himself and defining

himself/ wondrously illuminated/triumph over oppression/all you see is a human horror show/the pain . . . the pain/out of synch/collective amnesia/if you give up what's unique about you, you've lost your way/an ideal of heroic courage & a realistic acceptance of limits/it's not eccentricity that we're after, but revelation of beauty in a different form/the mystic hears the music within/ding, dong, the bitch is dead/ poet inhabits a transcendent, wondrously illuminated world/ writer who by penetrating into his own yearnings, & inner conflicts, discovered spirit of revolution can also lie within/ every day I have to redefine myself/ master of challenge issued to him or that he issues to himself/ an author who lacks clear national or ethnic identification/ individual spiritual odyssey/ transformation is only real when you share it/

to understand the love, care, compassion that's needed and not follow through is a crime/ relentless victimization of artist and homosexual/ salvation lay through art/ to reaffirm excellence/ I'm an atheist/ I like ben & jerry's, at ease with money/ unawakened man is not unified/ a chain of dreams/ heavy shots of fantasies, fascinations/

you can hear my heartbeat/ the statue of liberty/whenever i live with questions that the four walls of my apartment close in on me/ drop pebbles, ripple effects/ expression of his personal & immediate experience/ "true feeling" & in their directness & in their concern with what the singers call true feeling, the blues express a larger human reality/in the honesty of their emotion, is an insistent reminder that on either side of the race line, live other men& women, who find the same moments of pain & joy in the experience of life/personal response to the reality of experience/ it is the cry of pain, the shout of joy, the whisper of love, & the murmur of despair at separation and death/ wanderers at the edge of society/ complete break/community at crossroads but unmasking itself in light of the statue of liberty/ frightening and exhilarating/ try to carry him through/ if totality tells all, it doesn't end with going to sleep/

The writer grows desperate, quietly or not so quietly, as a failure or a has-been. Finally sets up plans that are pretexts. Great silence, with no end in sight. Surrenders listening. Wandering the ways of the world in search of adventure and glory. innocently making his way through a fallen and sterile world. a poet of loneliness, isolation, haunted & haunting. a poetry of free simplicity. enlarges our understanding. triumph of written word over death. everywhere but invisible in his work. journey from liberal apathy to a final commitment to the struggle for change in his own country. detached political concern. no salvation outside revolution. laboring in isolation. most powerful of all collected material: accumulated memories of childhood & adolescence. a generation still struggling to grow up. a voice demonic and proud. it is for them I write. in finding himself, he discovers a magnificent truth/ he's not at the mercy of anyone/ learn to play to no limits/ ransack the past/ I hear a song within me/ when I was about seven, knowing that I was different, sit here, horizon, the peculiarities of my behavior/ surf and surf/ in the shadows of the empire state building, the world trade centers & myself/ I begin this essay/sing to the seas, sing to the stars, sing to anybody who'd hear me, putting myself out there/solace/ every ten years, I change my mind/ this is where, one of us will have to come for solace/ Jan: Sweden's piers island of Alno yves: Haiti, Cayes' piers/ in search of solace and solitude/ in search of sex/ the last time somebody came in my ass/sensing danger yet defying it/ first time I had sex, in water/ on a windy, stormy day/ I hear the song within me: winds & waves/ I hear the music all around me/

the first time, swimming to this boat that had sunk/ almost died: scared of storms, winds & lightning/ counsel at Riis park, Ted swimming with the ashes/ embrace the things that scare me most/ I often come here by myself or with my partner/ nothing much happens here, looking, watching, listening, observing myself, losing myself in contemplation/anvil, mineshaft, peter rabbit, the ramrod, piers/

this is where i'll be if a cure, vaccine/cycle of life/ to hear the wind slap the window/as indispensable to our sense of time/ sad young men, hustling their dreams for a buck, for a fuck/ so often right in the midst of this noisy, dirty & lovely city that is new york, i often come searching for solace, myself/see a leaf blow up sky high/

if you are not a threat, that wouldn't be happening. no less than a catastrophe to wake us up. personal freedom: responsibility. do we deserve to be loved? wondrously illuminated. somebody coming to terms with himself & defining himself. all you see is a horror show . .

the pain . . . the pain is it crazy to be sensitive to the truth. the spirit is alive & well. do we wish to be portrayed that way. lost souls trapped in the American dream, if you give up what centers you, what's most unique about you, them you've lost your way. wanting an ideal of heroic courage & a realistic acceptance of limits. out of synch. whenever one starts, one reaches darkness. collective amnesia. i'm an atheist, i like ice cream, good hot sex, not necessarily in that order. nothing flashed. nothing clashed. unawakened man is not unified. discovers a magnificent truth: he's not at the mercy of anyone. spacious sense of reality. takes us so long to move into ourselves. he's on my case. he's on my ass. 3:00 A.M. is always showtime at the anvil. looking for better prospects in '90. i had a taste of honey. it's as if the dude went to school and learned to be cool. start from the little toe and move on up. i was addicted for 3 whole years. should have started to pray. i will always be busy when he dials my number. if it's 3:00 a.m. in the morning, i will say, oh, i was just stepping out. just as rich as the rockefellers but just ain't got that mind of cashflow. i got the grey out & got my braids extended. today you begin the task of writing life as it was happening. nothing is. because everything is a thought first then registered on paper. each moment brings its own turning point: artistic self-identification. literature does not save. in trying to understand an artist's life, one looks to his childhood. when his political consciousness was raised, a traumatic period. art meant to tell the truth. cost of living lies and price one pays. I am an eye. out of a hunger. personal affairs come before a sense of patriotism. power to move people. world of memories. writer can't be saved while writing. deaths on the horizon. artist's responsibility to society. a civilization is defined by the dreams it renounces. to remember and assess his position. unlike a musician or a painter, a writer needs a language. obvious and not very interesting, until question which language. Our century is littered with examples of writers who have had to make a choice to stick to or abandon their mother tongue. Almost more poignant than these is the case of a writer whose language is all around him & who at the same time is driven away from his language by political rather than personal considerations.

revolutionary is an extremist. service to the truth is among writer's highest concerns. fiery depths. revolution is not a religion, it lacked saints, prophets & martyrs. all or nothing. bomb-throwing terrorist. revolutionary terrorist committed supreme act of human will & human power killing indiscriminately in the belief that there are no innocent people in a corrupt society. The artist recognized the criminal or revolutionary anarchist-terrorist as romantic individual rebel who set himself proudly & defiantly against, above & beyond the laws & who embodied one of the possibilities of which artist & poet dreamed of, that of going to the limits of his being regardless of consequences. His gesture was beautiful. revolutionary artist: violent redeemer. transform the world, change life. birth of new idea, a new way of feeling. imperative for artists to be revolutionaries. preferred blood to ink. a call to action, a call to consciousness. when intellectual culture of a people & the customs & needs resulting from it are no longer in harmony with old political institutions, a necessary struggle arises against the latter which brings about a change in these institutions. salvation lay through art. poetry found in political action. for a storm or nothing. poet as rebel not revolutionary. never evaded writer's social responsibility. triumph over oppression/ ask question, be the question. writer who by penetrating into his own yearnings, inner conflicts, discovered that the spirit of revolution can also lie within. responsibility of choice & decision. rebirth is the basic need of revolutionary spirit. private overthrow of selfhood. violent upheavals are necessary to bring human spirit to entirely new purposes. what the world needs is a few crazies. creation rather than reaction. thrill of agitation & commotion. revolution is a terrifying yet wonderful apocalyptic prelude to salvation. regeneration of mankind. live your life as the deed instead of the doer.

salvation is preceded by dreadful punishments & catastrophes. engaged: empowered. never wish to create something that's not the holy in me. difference between forwarding the action & being a windbag. writer becomes master of challenge issued to him or that he issues to himself. know what's about to be written is about to be written. a criterion for excellence. commitment rather than feelings. an author who lacks clear national or ethnic identification, a man who confesses that everyday, he has to redefine himself. to transform every experience, predicament.

sure i get the blues, i learned how to snap out of them. if you don't like risk, you're looking for comfort. possibility lives in our language. one does not make possibilities by explaining, describing, or giving tips, but by declaring, by being committed. the promise lives in the word and in the action. that kind of innocence, you don't trade. unimaginable lives. dungeons of low self-esteem, archaic stereotypes, & selfish non-participation in the gay political struggle. inhabits a land he helped to create. most of us relegate our lives to looking good. we're rather resigned, living life in the space left after we're convinced that our lives don't make a difference. your fear of loneliness and rejection matches theirs. an artist in the process of creating. a gay black in search of himself.

love makes being alive worthwhile. paradise of spirit wherever are reborn. escapist petit bourgeois shit. crying is not the pain. pain happened before. the other excuse is that the term gay does not apply to me. straights are allowed a variety of images a clean canvas where the artist paints his future. tease ourselves with delusions. strip language down to its roots. sense of largeness and leisure. something that lifts us above the everyday. meditate on the music. liberation means no longer to permit death to have the last word on life, no longer to let death determine all our acts and attitudes through a fear of being dead. purpose is not to relate what has passed but to dominate what is to come. ritual cannot exist without some practical purpose. possession is a crisis within the life of the mind. the cross is never a masochistic symbol.

Christian hope looks not to the cross but to the crucified. to go to one's Ka means to return home to the land of the ancestors, to die. poetry is what defines the self. I love words. i love people most. a vision of human existence in an agnostic age. past is always a point of departure into a future that's always open. one knows who god is and who man is only when he hopes, when he bases his life on the unfathomable as his salvation. whoever abandons himself to what is unfathomable abandons himself to his salvation. presumption and despair in the same way refuse to abandon themselves to what is unfathomable. it's your milk that's making me sick. mother with cancer; a gay son with aids. live with a deaf lover & a puppy. imagine the future: a blur. illusions that didn't work. pretensions were dropped. uncertainty as a way of life. cut the roots that had once sustained him. guilty of subversive action. living on the edge, never losing balance. guided by moral intelligence, active social sense, or ethical thought. wake up to a world of wonder. puzzle over predicaments. strange things that happen coincidentally/ when Michael Evans died, a bag of ash, passed around/ an emotional outpour that was never reproduced on stage/ we are all in crisis/ we all have acquired immune deficiency syndrome/ if you have a lover, then why are you out? the best times have been with people who have lovers/ don't question what happens when you know two lovers, one happens to be your best friend who doesn't tell his lover that he's HIV positive/ i've questioned that if so and so were lovers for ten years, how come they didn't have joint accounts? epidemiology and demographics of AIDS/ HIV is disruptive . . . it disrupts the smooth flow of your life, living with questions, and we all want easy answers that alleviate our misery. i've kept myself alive by being open, by acknowledging the too real possibility of my dying young/ AIDS is but one of the many problems we face as a society/ it did not make me an activist/ my therapist keeps insisting that i display anger. i'm past that/ it's an overwhelming sense of mourning that never eases up/ use our poems as weapons to fight for our survival/ that fueled my artistic drives by its idiocy, pretense, bushshit/ there are no easy answers but the least we owe each other is trust and honesty/ censorship does not equal silence/ the one good thing about AIDS is that it doesn't discriminate/ it's fear/ fear of the unknown/ fear of havoc/ fear of losing control/ just because i'm different doesn't mean that i can't access power/ i know the pain of leaving my lover on a stretcher in a hallway in an emergency room/ i know the pain of watching friends deteriorate/ sensing the disease acting up in my nerves, my mouth, my lymphs/ i can sit on my terrace, look down at the avenue & see a dozen young men in one hour pass by, gaunt and frail, lesion-covered/ there are days when i've laid on the floor, no strength to get up/ as if the ground had a right to swallow me up right then and there/ burying David with a copy of brother to brother. burying redvers with other countries/ terror is a syndrome which like bleeding black bulls can act up/ always blaming whites for our

214

troubles/ the CDC is just estimating the extent of this crisis/ the famous choreographer, the famous designer, the famous playwright, director who die of blood diseases so rare that they don't have a name/ conspiracy of silence/ those mutual life insurance beneficiaries/ don't we love each other/ can't i risk my life for you/ two and a half years ago i met a man on christopher street/ i told him i was HIV positive/ he left me and took the bus, got off the bus at the next stop, walked to me, apologized, and said "let's go home." the first new year's eve after i found out, i was rejected twice that night/ i wanted excitement/ the thrill that a new year's eve is supposed to bring/ the gratefulness that indeed i was alive and relatively well/ we are all turned on by certain characteristics/ without question i acknowledge my own responsibility regarding this disease/ in 1991, why should we accept the fact that people are seroconverting? disruption to our sexual lives/ facing discomfort/ i once asked my mother, what would you do, if ten, twenty years from now, i'm dead, jan is dead, and millions are dead, and then on the news is came that this was a man-made virus/ what do you mean she kept asking/ what would you do i kept pushing her/ then she finally admitted that she'd be part of a revolution/ i kissed her and said "don't let me down." enter the church and the Gregorian chants/ crying for the faith that i lost/ the non-questioning innocence naivete/ if you're gay, it's at the expense of your blackness/ the role we are playing in our own victimization/ what do we, what can we make of all this suffering, it's nothing new, a different form/ scatters its artists to the wind/ vulnerability in terms of mortality/ the moon gives the city a glare/ is there poetry in all this? it's always good to look back, then keep moving on/ reached out for the greater good/ just as many folks go into medicine for the money and prestige, the same rule applies to folks going into AIDS/ not abandon ship, but all board/ the changing times when no one is watching, and you have to swallow your pills. know the pain of closing a friend's eyes/ know the pain of bearing witness/ Earvin Magic Johnson's announcement of his HIV antibody status last November triggered a reaction in the gay press similar to that of even well-meaning whites when blacks move into their neighborhoods. glad that they are advancing but not in my neighborhood/ the politics of AIDS are going to make strange bedfellows/ the phenomenon of gay men who refuse to get tested so as not to rock the boat, so they won't be put in the uncomfortable position of having to tell their sexual partners about their HIV status/ Freddie Mercury, Rock Hudson/ magic johnson simply happens to be the most famous person with HIV in the world/ a selfish knee-jerk reaction/ how many are not coming out/ While we rant against politicians' lies, we must do so against artists' lies. certain aspects of his relationship can be discussed (in good taste the one that ultimately destroyed your physical relationship with a man you loved. all facets of our lives. people who come out and find that they are still loved by most. I have to acknowledge the brutal cases when people have been rejected. owned by the public. yes you do have rights, but the right is to lie. exposed. & when people discover that you are lying, people are under no obligation to participate in your lie. not just great art but a great man. Before anything else, we are human beings. to be famous means to be naked. if your consciousness is raised, you will fight against lies which are the roots of oppression. It doesn't have to take martyrdom. They would have gotten more support. people would have realized that these artists are living on borrowed time. life-threatening situation. Nureyev, Robert Joffrey, and Alvin Ailey, Choo San gooh. the thought police. dismiss as outrageous. What outrages me are lies. the basic principle of outing is not an adherence to meanness, but to the truth. lies create more lies and ultimately lead us into chaos. take whatever from the bible and disregard the rest. amend the bible just as we did the constitution. artists who receive public money, unlike civil service workers whose daily works they don't copyright. if you know for sure, and not just guessing that you are HIV positive, i refuse to wear a red ribbon. How can you be violated by the truth. You are actually liberated. in fact i question the validity of their art, whether they were real or just one more fabricated lie and illusion. I'd be willing to bet. although I have always been a proponent of outing, I had never come face to face with one who had been outed. to demystify gayness and AIDS as something as natural as the air we breathe. because of your discomfort with the truth, I have to continue to be discriminated. i used to think that the disease would ease my rage. unlike other groups AIDS cuts through all barriers. what if they quarantine? money can be better spent for education and prevention. Part of the under-funding comes from the fact that they don't know the extent of the crisis. puzzling over my predicaments. writing my memorial. the Yves my family knew and those my friends and a certain amount of the public knew. a certain balance between the dead person's family, the friends, & the deceased's wishes. the different sides of my personality i showed in public, the high class & the vulgar the drag queen, the leather queen. I have seen beautiful memorials. Simply ones. i thought about having none but my wish would be broken. communality. give people a chance to come together in your memory. solid romantic notion that if jan were to die, i had to follow right after. as if to prove that we really loved each other. the control queen. Just as i have controlled certain events in my life, i also want to control what happens to me after i'm dead. this is exactly why some of us fled the tyranny of our families. my first initiation to AIDS as a GMHC buddy. one haitian sent back home to die, ex-saint worker/ lots of mothers & lovers/ lots of sadness & lots of hope and faith. witness to my weakness/ jan couldn't be bothered with funerals or memorials/ his focus is on fighting the myriad of opportunistic infections that get him sick/ i do want to discuss my dying and my death/ miracles of nature/ ate a plate of pasta with garlic & whole grain bread. for better or for worse jan and i met five days after reagan was elected president. your son won't get to heaven if he doesn't wish to get there. it takes so long to move into one's self always evolving and revolving. tragedy demands a calm despair. promise of community. guided by moral intelligence, active social sense, or ethical thought. when used as a message not a punishment. power to move people if it's true. not about what i ought to do so. what i ought to be. harness his central concerns. i often come to the piers/ this is where after closing joe's and david's eyes, we went. to hear their voices. language of symbols shared by the community. "art is a way of telling the truth." artist is a model for future generations. transforming the self & society. startled by the image in the mirror. learning involves fear and awe.

Plays

Risin' To The Love We Need

[a multimedia theater piece]

THE TIME

june 28th, 1980/ eve of gay liberation day/

THE CHARACTERS

FRANCINE: *40 years old black drag queen/ elegance in the extreme/ a singer who has gotten nowhere/ extravagant & plays a mean guitar/ four gardenias in her hair/ loves the color red/*

ASSOTTO: *26 years old light-skinned haitian writer/ wears black/ exotic in his beads, braids, feathered earring etc./ he is somewhat effeminate/*

BILLY: *35 years old, muscle-bound, very sexy prototype of black hustler/ excellent acrobatic disco dancer/ bald-headed & goes for whites/*

MILES: *19 years old knock-out beauty/ very dark-skinned & angular/ like a cat, ready to attack/ father complex in the men he picks for lovers/*

SUNNI: *31 years old blond hustler, pusher, dope dealer/ all around con man/ mr. know-it-all/ on roller skates, he carries a huge cassette player & plays the music loud/*

SPIRIT: *she of the dream, the love we need/ to be played by an androgynous-looking, black female dancer/ she's holder of the magic/*

EXTRAS: *two or three walk-ons/*

THE SET

the piers/ a no-man's land at the end of christopher street in new york city/ a sexual meeting ground/ a place where one can also sit by

223

the river & feel at peace with the universe/ high atop some steps, up
center stage, we find an old arm-chair: FRANCINE's throne/ upstage
right, a dilapidated building where people go in & out, seeking plea-
sure & adventure/ upstage left, we see the newark skyline/

ACT 1
(darkness/the curtains are drawn/ the SPIRIT casts spells on stage/
spotlight on FRANCINE, frozen in a josephine baker pose at the back
of the auditorium, carrying a guitar & suitcase)

FRANCINE: keeping contact with my wits, that's what i've been up
to/ not that jive-turkey i left, twisted on speed in that rathole i'm
paying, swearing i'd be back/ the cat leaned on me like it was rock/
i'm standing here pissed & i know i don't deserve this/ infinity's
where i'm off to

(we hear ASSOTTO chant from the stage although he remains invisi-
ble/ same goes for the others)

ASSOTTO: with my backbone

MILES: my piggy bank with the three pennies & the broken wishbone

BILLY: ghosts coming up in my cum

ASSOTTO: all my voodoo dolls

MILES: pretty flowers

FRANCINE: my little blue bird

MILES: angels & saints

FRANCINE: my incensed colored candles

ASSOTTO: memories drumming spells

FRANCINE: my juju

BILLY: & my mojo

FRANCINE: taking all that's real & holy to me/

(follow-up spotlight picks up FRANCINE as she proceeds down the aisle, drawn into the SPIRIT's magic & singing)

I AM OFF WITH MY MAGIC
STUMBLING ON BROKEN BOTTLES
LEAPING TO THE CRYSTAL BALL
BUT NEVER COMING BACK

(as FRANCINE steps onstage, both she & the SPIRIT bow to each other)

you children wondering what kind of creature i am/ all that color & them beads

(MILES is seen seated on the edge of the boardwalk, facing the hudson river, his back to the audience)

moaning in the middle of the street, spitting wishes in the hudson/ at times, i am baffled/ am i acting up or just nuts? cause i need no more attention/ what with these pretty rosy lips/ silky eyebrows i pluck & brush/ sensitive eyes/ look at them long delicate fingers/ all this honey in them hips/

(ASSOTTO is seen downstage left, pencil & pad in hand)

can't overcome what i am/ a treat/ this is me, the swish, good slow grooves, quick wit, camp, hot style & i sure feel mighty real, fully

225

aware of my identity/ ain't frightened by it one bit/ beauty's in the eyes of the beholder/ a high-colored queen, coming from a different standard/ ain't always easy on the eye/

(BILLY is seen upstage right, at the entrance to the piers)

wishing to freeze in time or go back to 1969, my vintage year, i mourned that last birthday of mine with a quart of gin/ everybody thought i'd o.d., slit my wrists, jump in front of the i.r.t. or all that front-page daily news shit but tonight, june 28th 1980, this forty year old is going to spread her legs/ does this ass seem familiar? baby, if love's what you're aiming for, this lover's got a glorious dream/

(as FRANCINE plays the guitar & sings, the SPIRIT dances)

FRANCINE: ALL OF YOU GATHER NOW
WE GONNA GO ON THIS BEAUTIFUL TRIP
ALL OF YOU GATHER NOW
WE GONNA GROW ON THIS BEAUTIFUL TRIP
KNOW WHERE WE BEEN
KNOW WHAT WE SEEN
IN OUR DREAMS

(the SPIRIT sprinkles magic dust on FRANCINE)

DREAMS

(the SPIRIT sprinkles magic dust on MILES who reacts but stays seated)

DREAMS

(the SPIRIT sprinkles magic dust on BILLY)

DREAMS

*(the SPIRIT sprinkles magic dust on ASSOTTO/ the others join
FRANCINE in singing)*

LIFT UP OUR SOULS
& STRIVE FOR ALL OUR DREAMS
& THRIVE IN ALL OUR DREAMS
GOTTA BELIEVE IN OUR GOALS
REDEEM OUR DREAMS

*(MILES watches BILLY go inside the piers, then he sits, facing the river/
ASSOTTO walks downstage right to FRANCINE)*

ASSOTTO: my my my! that was quite high/ that was quite fine,
Francine/

FRANCINE: nothing's going to keep this universal gal in the gutter/
Assotto, petit chou, how do you do?

(she kisses ASSOTTO on the forehead)

darling, when are we going to premiere that one-woman show you
wrote for me? DRAG-QUEEN BLUES, the story of my life/

ASSOTTO: girlfriend, i've been so busy with this collection of
poetry/

FRANCINE: good! heist yourself & read me one/ give me some of
that grand flair of yours/

ASSOTTO (sits at FRANCINE'S feet)
before i read, i should fill you in on a few things/ you see, in 1967,
when we were still living in haiti, my father was a captain in the

227

army/ he got involved in some military coup against papa doc
duvalier which failed/ we had to go underground for a few days/
we finally got out of the country on a boat/ the trip wasn't so bad
though/ two weeks later, we landed in fort lauderdale where they
granted us asylum/

FRANCINE: how on earth did you manage to get by the immigration
folks so easy/ look at what's happening these days with all them
refugees in detention camps/

ASSOTTO: we were well off & we came with money/ my father had connections in new york/ so we settled in brooklyn where the poem is set/

FRANCINE: even way back then, i remember there were lots of talk
in the black community, how uppity caribbean folks could be/ sometimes, i be strolling down eastern parkway & i hear all those accents,
i think i'm in another country/

*(she & ASSOTTO laugh, then he checks his pad & puts it aside/ on the
screen, a slide of the house where ASSOTTO grew up is projected)*

ASSOTTO: <u>REMEMBRANCE</u>

we lived in a two-story brownstone on atlantic
addicts & alcoholics squatted on one side/
this baptist church sanctified the neighborhood
each sunday with screams
songs
shouts
testimonies
tambourines

foot-stomps & hand claps/
the daisies i planted were such a soft touch/

228

straight A's
couldn't play ball
ran like a girl
perfumed with mother's cologne
practiced piano daily
wrote poetry
i was the type of sixteen year old
folks saw
thought quick something didn't click/
mother's favorite
i never misbehaved like ti-claude & frero
my older brothers/
didn't stay out late like they did/
she & i once picked up my father & brothers
in the car, father asked what i'd been up to/
i told him the truth/
i helped my cousin maryse dress her dolls/
right in the middle of the brooklyn bridge
he stopped the car
& knocked me out cold/
ti-claude & frero discussed ways
to change me from being a massisi/
often mother took me in her lap
told me not to worry/
we all waited for a miracle/

(the SPIRIT mimes ASSOTTO's words)

after much study in a mirror
i decided a hundred push-ups a day
would do in this sissy in me/
i'd be admired like all jocks/

guys kept ganging up/
split purple lips
eyes puffed black
red-scarred hands
i found my way home
smashed the mirror/

(FRANCINE plays the song "Remembrance" softly with her guitar)

took me months before i found baldwin
at the library/
million others out there/
i read vengefully/
spent every penny on xerox copies
collected all i could
called them my dreams/
at midnight
when the house hushed
i fetched my dreams from the closet
piled them
higher than the ceiling
higher than the empire state building/
hemmed in piles sky-high
i rocked myself to sleep
clutching a dream close/
one afternoon
busy with the grill in the garden
father shouted at me
"ti gacon, kite pran main sou ou
pral beat sissy shit ca outta your system/ "
i ran to my room
ransacked
looked out the window
my dreams up in smoke/

(smoke engulfs the SPIRIT who dances a requiem)

the tears shaken off my head
were not enough to assuage
the fire that raged in my heart/

*(ASSOTTO touches the crushed SPIRIT who again comes to life/the
SPIRIT picks up the imaginary ashes & stuffs them in a red bandanna)*

that night
i picked up those cold ashes/
a million stars as witness
i yelled
"ca yo papa
these were my dreams you burned/
they'll never die"

*(FRANCINE stops playing the guitar/ the SPIRIT rolls the bandanna
& ties it around her head)*

& i split/

*(FRANCINE plays the last seven notes of REMEMBRANCE as the
SPIRIT dances triumphantly then exits/
FRANCINE takes ASSOTTO in her arms/ the mood is broken when
we hear a voice rap from the aisle: "I GOT THAT GRASS THAT'LL
KNOCK YOU ON YOUR ASS/ IT'S GOOD FOR YOUR HEAD BEFORE
YOU GO TO BED/ MAKES YOU SCREAM BEFORE YOU DREAM/ "
BILLY comes out of the piers to check what's happening/ he jumps
down to greet SUNNI who rollerskates on stage/ a huge cassette
player is strapped over his shoulders, playing the song "Born To Be
Alive" by Patrick Hernandez)*

BILLY: Sunni, my man!

SUNNI: chief, i thought you'd be at the mineshaft by now/

BILLY: man, i'm down on my last five/ seems like things are picking up around here/ what you got for me?

SUNNI: tuinols, demerols, ups, downs/ name it, claim it/

BILLY: i need some acid bad tonight/

(SUNNI extends his hand, waiting for BILLY to pay him)

come on man, i'll pay you next week/ i shot this hot new flick & the guy's going to give me the dough tomorrow/

SUNNI: i heard that one before/

BILLY: hey Sunni, it's me, Billy, your old buddy/ don't i always pay you back, man/

SUNNI: alright/ take this yellow jack . . .

(SUNNI hands him a pill & his army canteen)

& fuck with all your might/

(skates down where ASSOTTO & FRANCINE stand/
ASSOTTO reacts somewhat negatively to SUNNI but FRANCINE is
quite pleased)

no need for serious or mysterious looks/ i know you'se a queen but darling . . .

(SUNNI lifts FRANCINE'S dress)

you'se taking this royalty thing a bit too far/

FRANCINE: (*blows a kiss to SUNNI*) long time no seen the mean machine/ how have you been?

SUNNI: highhhh!

FRANCINE: i bet/ SUNNI, you take food stamps?

(SUNNI takes the food stamps, counts them & hands FRANCINE a few joints/ MILES comes down center stage)

SUNNI: (*skates past MILES*) boy! when they talk about black beauties, i want one just like you/

(MILES gives him cold shoulders)

BILLY: (*to SUNNI as he gives him the canteen*) don't he look like he's from another planet?

SUNNI: yeah, what's with all this schizoid make up? ain't them buns for fun?

(SUNNI pinches MILES's behind/
FRANCINE lights a joint/
BILLY grabs SUNNI's sunglasses from him/
SUNNI is more & more intrigued by MILES who walks away from him)

BILLY: (*flashes the glasses at FRANCINE*) smile! you'se on camera!

(FRANCINE strikes another pose, puffing smoke in BILLY'S face/ she tries on the sunglasses)

SUNNI: (*removing the sunglasses from FRANCINE*) come on, you don't need them sunglasses/ i watch you catch crotches half-a-mile away/

FRANCINE: two miles!

SUNNI: (*to ASSOTTO who walks by*) walking awfully slow darling/ whatever it was, must have been quite fine/

(ASSOTTO who is more relaxed, takes the joint from FRANCINE who sniffs on poppers that BILLY gives her)

if you're going to say you'se gay, go all the way/ leave them troubles behind/ let this superb herb blow your mind/ do it slow/ do it fast/ feel it flow/ make it last/ satisfaction guaranteed/

(joints & poppers are passed/ they all dance/ ASSOTTO & FRANCINE do the latin hustle/ they sing, whistle & carry on except for MILES who watches them)

FRANCINE: (breaks away) this is pier 46, with its army of tricks on trips, standing by for the thrill to combat your secrets, maneuver your drives, service your fantasies/

(slides, depicting various sexual activities that go on inside the piers, are rolled fast)

BILLY: pier 46, where you shall be what we wish you to be/ ALIIIVE!

(it becomes a chorus started by BILLY)

ALL: BE ALIVE! BE ALIVE! BE ALIVE! BE ALIVE! IT'S GOOD TO BE ALIVE . . .

FRANCINE: warning/ only

234

(bows to the audience & points to MILES)

the beautiful

(indicates ASSOTTO)

the bold

(indicates BILLY & SUNNI)

& the big shall survive/

(the instrumental part of "Boogie Oogie Dancin Shoes" by Claudja Barry comes on the cassette player)

SUNNI: *(to FRANCINE)* did i ever tell you that story when me & Billy went to the ice-palace?

FRANCINE: the ice-palace? no!

(the SPIRIT appears in a white mask & dressed in man's clothes/ she's the bouncer at the ice-palace/ she lets BILLY, SUNNI in but asks BILLY for i.d.'s/ BILLY who is used to this sort of treatment, takes his i.d.'s from his pocket & is let in/ BILLY climbs the steps & starts to dance wildly/ SUNNI narrates)

SUNNI: rumor had it that friday night at the ice-palace that this crazy niggah on the platform, dancing up a storm, was a real-live ghetto niggah/ only niggahs from down bed-stuy or up lennox grooved that good/ east-side black queens had classy moves/ this muthah was breaking in them tighter than tight white jeans tucked in red snake skin cowboy boots with spurs, a white t-shirt that read in red "I AM THE BOSS," this red felt hat while a gold star sparkled on his left ear lobe/

FRANCINE: give it more flint Billy boy/ hit it/

ASSOTTO, SUNNI & FRANCINE: (*in unison*) WORK THAT BODY!
WORK THAT BODY! WORK THAT BODY! WORK THAT BODY!

FRANCINE: (*to SUNNI*) oh my honey, what in the world did you give him?

SUNNI: just another niggah acting up, the tired-looking, tired-mov-
ing white queens cracked/ when they bumped, he freaked/ when they
freaked, he rocked & did the patty duke/ when they tried those two,
he laughed as he blessed them with sweat/ there was more than one
upset sissy when he tore up his t-shirt, beat his chest & growled,
flashing through the crowd brashly/ those stiff sterile queens scattered quick, fanning stuck-up noses with limp jeweled hands/ BILLY
did somersaults, cartwheels, carried on with all kinds of acrobatics
then split in the middle of the floor/ when he got up, took off his
hat, smoke curled round his head like a halo/ his cocoa-oiled chest
glowed in the dark/ he whirled, whirled & whirled, lost in another
world, his for the night/

    (led by BILLY, they execute the line hustle, singing with Claudja
        Barry/ MILES watches them from his corner)

ALL: BOOGIE OOGIE DANCIN SHOES, KEEP ME DANCIN ALL
NIGHT/ BOOGIE OOGIE DANCIN SHOES, MAKE ME QUEEN FOR A
NIGHT/

    (satisfied that he brought aliveness to the group, SUNNI waves to
        them & goes inside the piers, taking the music with him)

FRANCINE: (*drops on the chair*) don't we act up when we're down/

BILLY: whenever my spirit gets low, i dress my wildest/

(slides of BILLY in his costumes are projected)

leather/ chaps, boots, cap, vest, keys dangling down my left pocket, i
check the spike/ bud in hand, i feel the atmosphere/

ASSOTTO: but Billy, that's your name right?

FRANCINE: whatever became of my manners? i forgot to introduce
you two/ Billy, this is Assotto, a poet with lots of flair/ Assotto, this
is Billy, porn star EXTRAordinaire

ASSOTTO: *(to BILLY)* what i wanted to tell you is that who you are is
not valued in those bars/

(FRANCINE fans BILLY who wipes himself with his t-shirt)

BILLY: *(flexes his muscles)* what you look like, that's the magic/

FRANCINE: plasticity & stuff like that, these days taken so much
at heart/ once, this village was for real/ everywhere, a family affair/
one could feel the power of the place/ the village was the village for
everybody/ queens shared space/ all over now, attitudes/ it's a bad
joke/ i declare christopher street a disaster zone/

(BILLY dismisses FRANCINE as if she's exaggerating)

ASSOTTO: & girl, we are left for the color/ they all look alike, those
clone-affected jaded white kids, never growing/

FRANCINE: don't they be degrading me cause i feel like dressing in
silk & these sure ain't no fuck-me boots/

ASSOTTO: *(to BILLY)* you can grow a moustache, carry color-coded
hankies, work out at the y., you still come up spades/

FRANCINE: thank you/

ASSOTTO: i learned that the hard way cause i never knew what racism was until i came to this country & here, it didn't matter that my grandfather was vice-president of haiti, or that we had five servants/

FRANCINE: *(points to MILES)* so strange to see pretty boys like him searching/ with all he got i wonder for what/

(the SPIRIT takes a picture out of her corset & holds it above MILES's head)

MILES: as with so many of us, father was never there but daddy, your shadow's everywhere/ you are this immense black sky i aspire to/ all i breathe is fog i see in these precious pictures mother kept all these years/ i am your spitting-image, carbon copy/ america is full of slick black cats whose big dicks sire bastards/ america is full of black bastards who dream of daddy's big dick/ how i wait anywhere, wait for the day we meet, i shall kiss . . .

(the SPIRIT kisses the picture as SUNNI comes out of the piers/ SUNNI thinks that MILES is talking to him)

blow you away, muthah-fuckah/

(the SPIRIT tears up the picture & throws the pieces at the audience)

SUNNI: are you for real?

MILES: as real as can be/

BILLY: he must be on a new drug/

SUNNI: probably high on noxzema from all that moisturizing/

238

MILES: don't you pluck my last nerves or i'll straw-dog you/

SUNNI: is you serious?

MILES: as a heart attack/

BILLY: (*to SUNNI*) turn on the music, man/ later for miss dramatic here/

(*BILLY grabs SUNNI's cassette player as SUNNI tries to catch up with MILES who runs inside the piers/ SUNNI goes after him/ "Contact" by Edwin Starr is heard as BILLY dances*)

in the streets, sometimes, my eyes are sparkling flies that scatter across the skies, to bite another number's eyes/

FRANCINE: (*comes down to dance with BILLY*) i know all about them heavy-lidded glances enticing my tricks/

BILLY: no rush/ the eyes kiss & smile/ a good catch/ thanks to . . .

(*they grind & sing along with the song*)

EYE TO EYE CONTACT/ EYE TO EYE CONTACT/ EYE TO EYE CONTACT/
EYE TO EYE CONTACT, YOU & ME . . .

(*BILLY starts to strip down his pants/ ASSOTTO is busy, peeking into FRANCINE's suitcase out of curiosity*)

FRANCINE: (*pulls up BILLY's flyer*) mercy on sister's eyes/

BILLY: look who's talking/ hey Assotto, ever seen miss thing doing her thing on west street/

ASSOTTO: (*comes down with the suitcase*) first time i met the lady last fall, she was turning it out on tenth street at 4:00 A.M./

FRANCINE: darling, where are you going with my suitcase?

(*ASSOTTO got the idea to dress up FRANCINE like she does when she works the streets/ as ASSOTTO narrates the next story, he takes various things out of the suitcase, dresses FRANCINE & does her make up/ MILES comes out of the piers to watch the action*)

ASSOTTO: long blond tresses sprigged with gold, plucked eyebrows, purple mascara round the eyes to make them look large & luminous, cheekbones that won't quit, thick green flutters, chain-shaped silver pendants framing her coffee-colored full face, ruby reds & loads of rouge to hide the shaving marks, reeking of avon, she was bad/ the way she carried on waiting for a john, no one could tell that she was a he/

caped in flawless purple satin splashed with gold beads & trimmed with black ostrich, she leaned her six-foot frame against the fire-alarm pole, looking sexy in this hot pink dress, slit on both sides to the waist, sashed with a gigantic bow/

(*to BILLY*)

miss thing, she had seen such novelty in an issue of vogue which she'd picked up from the garbage can in front of waverly/ for an entire week, she slaved over the outfit/ gold fringes & paillettes were her own touch/

(*the SPIRIT walks across the stage with a banner that reads "THE HARASSMENT OF OUR QUEEN/ "
from then on, its story-theater of what could have happened to FRANCINE/
a fierce game of wits ensues between ASSOTTO & BILLY/ FRANCINE*)

240

is a checker, moved around by BILLY & ASSOTTO but the action is controlled by the SPIRIT who also enacts the sketches/ in the next one, the SPIRIT plays a cop & a judge)

BILLY: two weeks ago, hustling in the manhattan plaza garage, a cop snatched her out of her lover's arms, in the backseat of a '69 pinto/ he let the john go but whisked her to the queens' tank where some of the girlies, waiting months for a court date, fought with one another/ miss thing pleaded

FRANCINE: guilty

BILLY: each time she got busted/ that's why her record was long & messed up/ she'd agree to serve a week or 10 days at rikers/ that was the sure way out/ after all, she had no sugar-daddy/ she couldn't get a sympathetic lawyer & those johns to whom she brought so much love, they were of no help/

(the SPIRIT becomes the man at the bar in the next sketch)

ASSOTTO: she'd go to bars, strike up conversation with one of those too boozed up to hold his head straight/ the boy would gladly oblige & buy the lady a drink or two/ she'd lull him outside with sweet talk, promises of good times/ no money deal just free love/ she'd walk him along deserted streets to some hot-spring hotel/ he'd feel good, leaning against her strong shoulders, talking, crying about marital troubles/ soon as he'd smile, look at her through bleary eyes, she'd quickly pull out a blade & the unsuspecting john would say:

SPIRIT: take anything/ here/ leave me alone/

ASSOTTO: she would & she'd make it back to the bar in time to slip a bill in the bartender's pocket/ she had to support a silicone & hormone treatment/ S.S.I. just wouldn't do/ she was no queen made up for the night/ drag was her life/

FRANCINE: & honey, this shit's a trip/

(the SPIRIT acts the part of the porto-rican dude in the next sketch)

BILLY: things weren't easy/ good times were far away/ once, this portorican dude picked her up down delancey/ after she showed him her tongue's delight, she was not one of these high mighty queens one finds at gg's who say "do anything to me just don't touch my face: & well, after she nearly passed out from so much talcum powder & so much brut, he wanted to take her the normal way/ to make her feel his dick deep down like he had kept whispering/ lost in some fleeting fantasy, she didn't realize what he was up to till he screamed:

SPIRIT: MARICON! MARICON!

BILLY: she saw her dainties & g-string at her feet/ she barely got out of the car after much struggling & biting when he shot her in the back/ the bullet passed through her stomach, leaving a scar/ for weeks at bellevue, she joked with the nurses about her two belly buttons/

ASSOTTO: a shimmy here, a slimmer there, she advertised that stuff, casting come-on glances at the passing cars which caused church-going gals to pull up their windows fast & look the other way/ most of the guys though would do a double-dig/ one night, some poor slob crashed into a pole/

(the SPIRIT becomes the crazy white boy in the following sketch)

BILLY: as she posed, waiting to flag a car, she saw this crazy-look-ing white boy coming her way/ she took off her green spike pump

242

fast, brandished it in her right hand/ her left hand on her hip, cheeks sucked in, lips pushed out with a whistle, she stared straight at him, ready to strike/ he smiled, blew her a kiss while he walked by/

ASSOTTO: in the distance, she thought she heard a siren/ cosmetic intuition she calls it/ she tried to run to the piers & fell in a puddle/ hopping on one sandal, she dragged herself behind a parked volkswagen as a paddy wagon whizzed by/

FRANCINE: i ain't garbage to be swept off the streets whenever some goddamn pig feels like it/ the streets belong to the people & i am somebody/ next time you force me down on you, i'll bite it off/ no dough, no blow/

BILLY: she stood there till the siren sounded far away/ then, she sat on the edge of the boardwalk, all wrapped up in her cape, legs dangling in the air, smoking the last cigar from a pack this guard with whom she'd made it in jail had given her/ he had been nice to her, bringing her issues of ladies' home journal, reader's digest, once, pictures of his old lady which miss thing had begged him for/ each time they had gotten together, he had offered her ten bucks which she always refused, saying:

FRANCINE: just tell me i'm better than her

BILLY: he did, every single time/ she knew he meant it/

ASSOTTO: she stared for a long time at her reflection in the water/ the wind blew unkind/ as she raised her head, looking dead-ahead, she sang/

(the SPIRIT hands FRANCINE the guitar/ as FRANCINE plays & sings, the SPIRIT dances a very lyrical suite)

243

FRANCINE: I SIT HERE SO LONELY
AS TIRED AS CAN BE
& WATCH A BIRD FLY FREELY
IN THE SKY
I WISH I COULD GO UP
UP UP & FLY NON-STOP
LEAVE EARTH CAUSE I'M FED UP
& STAY HIGH

TO BREATHE FREE, TO BREATHE DEEP
SOMEPLACE WHERE I COULD FLEE
SOMEPLACE WHERE I WOULD BE
AT PEACE & BE ME
NO FEAR & NO WORRY
I AIN'T FEELING SORRY
TO BE FREE IN GLORY
IS MY CRY

TO BREATHE DEEP, TO BREATHE FREE
SOMEPLACE WHERE I COULD FLEE
SOMEPLACE WHERE I WOULD BE
AT PEACE & BE ME
SOMEPLACE WHERE I WOULD BE
AT PEACE & BE ME

(silence for a few beats then ASSOTTO & BILLY shout)

ASSOTTO & BILLY: hi miss thing!

ASSOTTO: girlfriend, what are you doing, singing sad songs on the
edge of the pier? you're going to fall in the water/ you need a good
stiff cocktail to perk you up/ come on, get up/

(FRANCINE stands up as the SPIRIT assembles FRANCINE's things &

244

puts them in the suitcase/ the SPIRIT then hides it behind the chair)

FRANCINE: oh, let's go to peter rabbit for a while/ Billy, you want to come with us/

BILLY: you go on/ i'll stick around here/
see you when we come back/

(ASSOTTO & FRANCINE exit down the aisle, through the audience/
MILES is on stage, alone with BILLY & the SPIRIT/ it's obvious that
MILES is attracted to BILLY who looks at him hesitantly then goes
inside the piers, taking the cassette player with him/
MILES, who is disappointed, sits on the chair/ the SPIRIT gestures
for the lights to dim)

END OF ACT 1

(15 minutes later/ MILES is seated on the steps/ the SPIRIT gestures for the action to resume/ wearing a tuxedo, top hat & juggling a cane, the SPIRIT forces MILES to exorcise the memories of his ex-lovers)

MILES: every man i fell for, greeted me with

(slide of lover #1 is projected/ he's holding the same cane that the SPIRIT juggles)

SPIRIT: pretty baby ease on down with daddy/ ease on/

(the SPIRIT taps MILES with the cane/ slide of lover #2 is projected/ he's wearing the same top hat as the SPIRIT)

child, worries don't become you/ smile/

(the SPIRIT tosses the hat away/ slide of lover #3 is projected/ he's dressed in the same tuxedo as the SPIRIT)

kitty cat, i got connections/ i'll make you a star/

(the SPIRIT takes off the jacket & taunts MILES like a toreador)

MILES: i heard them all/ it grieves that this past new-year's eve, not one of those suckers was by my side to toast even a cup of fresh coffee/

(MILES walks downstage)

hey, you failed me/ you failed to notice beneath this bitchiness is pain/ this softness in my eyes is hurt/ in eagerness, thinking i found love at last, i rushed, ass open wider than the sky/

(slide of lover #2 is projected again as the SPIRIT impersonates him)

SPIRIT: too much sugar, baby/

MILES: you said/

SPIRIT: heavy pressure/

(the SPIRIT blows a kiss to MILES then exits)

MILES: i had put my body on line, my whole soul into you/ i was a vision of loveliness in many a foolish faggot's life/ like a coat of fog, moving on/ in no way, shape or form, will i be used, misused or abused anymore/ raising some shit-head's standard then discarded for another/ i got body, beauty & brains/ hey, if it's desire for me you cherish, dig where you're at & dig you, i must/ hail this message loud & clear/ salvation's upon me/

(SUNNI comes out of the piers with his cassette player)

SUNNI: there you are foxy/ where you been hiding? don't you know the mean machine got no time for games/ Sunni gets what he wants when he wants it/ i want you now/ i must warn you, them black girls at peter rabbit just go wild for my white meat/ what's your sign, sweetie? you'se as serious as them cancers/ i sure would like to get your hot buns/

(he pinches MILES's ass/ MILES moves one step down)

why you jumpy? got to slow down, darling/ you ain't one them frozen fruits, is you? kiss me/

(the SPIRIT stands behind them/ MILES walks away & sees BILLY come out of the piers in open shirt, zipping his flyer)

MILES: faggots can get so caught up sexually, i'll bet they'll work their way into heaven measuring god's dick/

SUNNI: listen to her now/ say, when did you get in heaven to sit by the throne of god? come here, sweetie/

(SUNNI grabs MILES)

Sunni'll take you & give you something fierce/ this mean machine will light up your fire/ make you want to testify/

MILES: don't let me crush your hopes/ you may be a rooster but you ain't roosting me/

(SUNNI kisses MILES hard on the lips/ MILES kicks him in the groin/ SUNNI bends over in pain)

i'll beat you into bad health & out to a speedy recovery/

(MILES walks up center stage, wiping his lips)

SUNNI: sweetie, your dick has risen but it ain't got hard yet/ you hear me/ it just ain't hard/

BILLY: *(walks over to SUNNI)* you alright, man?

MILES: any planet with stars & sunsets, a rainbow & a moon, should have beautiful people/ often clouds form/ rain falls/ fog/ we shall be caterpillars, crawl through mud before we become butter-flies/ sylvester & two tons moaning low, can make me hypothesize myself straight into paradise with the man of my dreams/ the man who never was/ the man often i think can never be/ i remember when i was younger, late at night, mama would weave stories & melodies while her fingers made ripples on my back/ then, asleep fallen, i'd

dream such happy dreams/ mama was there/ now that i've grown
& she's gone, good days away seem blown but i carry on/ mama &
christ wish peace for me/ one day, the right man'll come along/ we
will love the way love was meant to be/

SUNNI: alright, miss chastity/ who needs this damn jive bout
dreams? dream you could rim this funky honky ass/ a broad here, a
dude there, what do i care? Sunni goes everywhere for the pleasure/
when these high-stepping skates take off down christopher street, i
bring the power back home, where it belongs/

*(SUNNI turns on his cassette player/ the instrumental of "Good
Times" by CHIC is heard)*

i am a magnet, with the ease that's been my trademark/ why should
i rush & climb up to anything? let skies, mountains & folks freak on
down to me/ everybody wants Sunni/ Sunni gives you nothing but
L-U-V/

*(the SPIRIT walks over to SUNNI who pays no attention to her as he
gropes his groin & moves to the beat)*

BILLY: i am the boss/ they told me i am the boss/ i fucked them/
they've fucked over me/ yet, i'm hanging onto this string of one-night
stands/

(BILLY turns the music off)

every night, kellers, sneakers, filled with numbers to look at/ many i
like/ some i lead on/ one to lay, leave for others to look at, like, lead
on, lay, leave/ so much fucking order/ been losing track/ Sunni, we
just can't keep feeding our sack & kick ass/ we got to succeed beyond
the copulation point/

SUNNI: you sure didn't look too unhappy when you were in there, screwing that child wild/

BILLY: those tricks been nothing but shit on this dick/ ghosts coming up in my cum/

(SUNNI walks away, tired of being sermonized/ the SPIRIT blocks him but he manages to get by her & goes inside the piers/ the SPIRIT follows him/ BILLY leans on the lamp post/ MILES paces back & forth downstage left, wanting to reach out to BILLY/ ASSOTTO & FRANCINE walk down the aisle to the stage)

ASSOTTO: i run my life/ make choices here & they're mine/ hell i thought was these million eyes beaconing me/ all roads lead to our conscience/ the curse/ i sure bless myself/ i am what i am: a niggah on a faggot trip/

FRANCINE: so-be-it/

(FRANCINE sits on the chair as ASSOTTO sits at her feet)

ASSOTTO: struggling for my space, i survive on a shoestring but i found strength to be assotto saint, a poet/ my crazy black gay rhythms will ring rough, years to come/

FRANCINE: *(lights her cigar)* critics will tell you this black gay trip ain't universal/

(specials on ASSOTTO & the SPIRIT who's seated in her corner, surrounded by various puppets)

ASSOTTO: two weeks ago, i showed up at this conference on gay images in the media/ i was giving them looks to kill in my dashiki, beads, braids & bandanna, feathered earring/

FRANCINE: child, you must have looked brutal/

ASSOTTO: you better believe it & i raised the issue of racism in the gay media/ i wanted them to justify why they do to us blacks what they don't wish the new york times to do to all of us gays/ this silly-looking queen said:

SPIRIT: (*holds a puppet*) according to what's printed in the program, we are not here to discuss racism & if we do, we might as well discuss the holocaust/

FRANCINE: honey, being black in america at times has been worse than a holocaust/

ASSOTTO: another one said:

SPIRIT: (*holds another puppet*) i'm sick of that black victim act/ go take est or something/

ASSOTTO: by the time sister was burning up/ some of them wanted to throw me out/ one even told me

SPIRIT: (*holds another puppet*) if you're so disgusted with things here, why don't you go back to whatever island you're from/

FRANCINE: shhhhhh . . .

ASSOTTO: this fiftyish, fifties-hairdo, affected queen screamed:

SPIRIT: (*holds another puppet*) when you people learn how to write proper english then we'll give you jobs/

ASSOTTO: that did it/ i kept cool & quoting ms colored girl ntozake shange i said:

SPIRIT: *(throws away the puppets)* I CAN COUNT THE NUMBER
OF TIMES I HAVE VISCERALLY WANTED TO ATTACK DEFORM 'N
MAIM THE LANGUAGE THAT I WAZ TAUGHT TO HATE MYSELF IN.
THE LANGUAGE THAT PERPETUATES THE NOTIONS THAT CAUSE
PAIN TO EVERY BLACK CHILD AS HE/ SHE LEARNS TO SPEAK OF
THE WORLD & THE SELF.

ASSOTTO: flushed some colorful sense in those fades' faces/

(the SPIRIT exits)

FRANCINE: ain't that a bitch/ every gay theater rejected that fine
performance piece you wrote for me/ me, the colorful queen of
christopher street who gave eleven of the best years of her life to gay
liberation/ gave her nothing in return/

ASSOTTO: these things tick me off/ whenever i look at a gay maga-
zine, we are only seen escorting some white queen to a concert, the
disco & of course the bedroom as if we blacks never get to enjoy gay
sex with each other/

FRANCINE: years back, when i first walked down christopher street
by all those salt & pepper couples, i used to whisper, what a wonderful world this is/ indeed, what a wonderful world it could be but i
tell you, this transition period's a whole different scene/ this rivalry
between black queens for the white child's developing into some
full-fledged war out here/

*(the SPIRIT drags SUNNI out of the piers/ she forces him to put on
the white mask she wore for the ice-palace scene)*

ASSOTTO: fighting each other like monkees after a banana/ what
for? some whites who can't come close to us as people/ you hear all
this jive how europeans are different, europeans are decent?

FRANCINE: oh dear/

(SUNNI dramatizes with the SPIRIT what ASSOTTO says)

ASSOTTO: last summer, i met this french photographer/ right there on christopher street, he snapped me & we hit it off quite quickly/

FRANCINE: i bet you did/

ASSOTTO: took me to this fabulous duplex in chelsea/ all kinds of antiques & sound system/ we drank pina coladas, listened to piaf, discussed lady koch & her racist politics, the tension between blacks & jews . . .

FRANCINE: that's some renaissance stud you had there/ these days, they're an endangered species/ most of these post-stonewall gals ain't well, honey/ all they want to talk about on sunday afternoons is last night's trick who's always the best they've ever had/ standing up in front of badlands so they can get a better one/ fire island & that new copa place which is for craps/ imagine going to a tea-dance & there's no tea/ i hear they're going to open the biggest disco in the world called the saint/ how appropriate a name/ for 20 bucks every saturday night, those queens will get to sanctify their asses/ membership went for a couple of hundreds/ the tragedy of gay society/ c'est la vie/ oh, don't let me go off, assotto/ i want to hear the rest of that story/

ASSOTTO: then around eleven, i was feeling good/ the dude was nib-bling my nipples, licking my chest, blowing soft sounds into my ears/

FRANCINE: i know how wine & songs can warm the heart/

ASSOTTO: we were high on this thing called target & girlfriend, target was on target/ i was so high & my pants were coming down/

253

suddenly i get hold of them because i never give myself to any guy, let alone a white guy, if he doesn't tell me what he finds most interesting in me/

FRANCINE: vanity personified or is it you got something to hide?

ASSOTTO: (*smiles but goes on*) i kept asking & he'd just smile, size my hard-on & try to take my pants down/ then, he signaled for me to follow him to the bedroom & he switched on the light/

SUNNI: voila! i love blacks/

(*on the screen, a collage of naked black guys is projected*)

ASSOTTO: there, on the wall, a thousand naked black guys & i was so surprised/

FRANCINE: why? all the white queens i know who are into blacks own extensive collections of their lovers' pictures/

ASSOTTO: well, i asked him about his preference for us blacks/ guess what he said?

FRANCINE: our cocks of course!

ASSOTTO: (*shakes his head*) when he was growing up on this farm in france, he had this black goat called bouba/ he used to snuggle against bouba/ our curly hair reminds him of bouba's & that i'm an exception since he doesn't usually go with light-skinned blacks/ we smell . . .

FRANCINE: cheri, mais tu blagues?

ASSOTTO: my hard-on went down/ he tried to stop me as i opened the door but i pushed him, turned around & said

SPIRIT: (*mimics a goat*) BAAAYE . . .

(the SPIRIT & SUNNI exit)

ASSOTTO: the gull! it amazes me how many of us blacks let ourselves be trapped in their kinky fantasies/

*(on the screen, a picture of BILLY which is part of the collage is
zeroed in)*

including you know who/

(indicates BILLY)

talks black, sleeps white/

BILLY: man, i mostly go with whites/ i have never denied that &
i will not bother finding a reason why either/ i'll leave that to you
writers & shrinks who can never accept something can just be/ have
an orgasm on me/ for that matter, have a second coming too/

ASSOTTO: you are nothing but one of these lazy classy niggahs running all over town, shining each other on, out for joy rides with these
white fat cats, mama's inheritance up their middle-class asses/

BILLY: what did you say?

ASSOTTO: you heard me loud & clear/

FRANCINE: hold it/ i said hold it/ we're just getting to know one
another & already we're fighting/ black gay folks haven't even begun
to say hello, how can we wave goodbye? let us chill our tempers &
hold onto our manners/

BILLY (*to FRANCINE*) i like him/ i do but he got all this blackness business messing bad with his mind/

ASSOTTO: you got some nerve buster, talking to me about blackness/ you lost yours way back/

BILLY: my blackness is here/ it's always been here & will be here till the day i die/ it's nothing but . . .

(BILLY pinches his skin)

this/ some folks are born black, others white/ some like chocolate, others like vanilla/ smart ass like you want me to believe there's more to it/ i can't buy that/

ASSOTTO: how can you stand here & honestly think you are not different? how can you?

BILLY: you're damn right, i'm different/ ain't better or less than the dude next door/ i just am me, Billy & i'm never going to live my life like some defense mechanism or a reflex action to whatever straights or whites do/ no siree/ Assotto, the goddamn truth is you can't live your life without them/ your gayness is always viewed in relation to their straightness/ you'll never be satisfied to be black in a room all by yourself/ got to have whites so you can prove how different & better you are/ i saw that damn play of yours last year/ nothing but pain, anger & blame, blame, blame/ expecting apologies & all that sorry for yourself tired crap/

ASSOTTO: how dare you/

BILLY: don't get me wrong man/

ASSOTTO: don't you touch me/

BILLY: don't get me wrong man/ i admire your guts/ you were the first man, the first to write an all-black gay play, but Assotto, those characters weren't living on that stage/ that's surviving & i want to live/ l-i-v-e/ i ain't no fool/ where i'm at now, i ain't getting what i need & nobody but me, Billy, got Billy in this mess/ ok? i'm getting my shit complete & blacks, browns, yellows, i'm open to the possibilities of loving, fears, faults & all the rest/

(BILLY wants to exit but the SPIRIT stops him)

ASSOTTO: no honky can ever give you the love you need/ they're either your age or younger/ all they see is this piece of high-caloric meat to treat themselves to occasionally/ or they're a bunch of old queens looking like shit & ready for geriatrics/ old white queens who paid us blacks no mind when they were young & could trick with their own kind/ now watch them rush & grab us/ definitely not this one/ i'll take a third-rate black cat who means well anytime before i take a first-rate white/

FRANCINE: *(fans ASSOTTO)* easy, easy honey/ don't you let bitterness upset your pressure/ they done be victimized by a million myths/ it's our duty, our duty i repeat, to let them see us, feel us as we really are/

ASSOTTO: *(sits on the steps)* they're not worth the pain/ to be dehumanized into a dick is far more damaging than to be discriminated/

MILES: *(moving closer to the group)* your own kind can crucify you faster & harder than any other/

FRANCINE: thank you/ in '68, when politics got real messy . . .

(slides depicting the turbulence of 1968 are projected/ the assassinations, the chicago democratic convention, anti-war & civil rights demonstrations along with FRANCINE doing her thing)

& keeping silence meant illness & ulcers, i went to join them pan-
thers as i am black, spirited & committed/ wouldn't you know them
motherfuckers started this disgrace to the race, discredit to the
cause bit/ actually they threatened to pistol-whip this sissy shit out
of me/ that whole situation built up my anger even more/ i tell you,
for a goddamn year, i felt like an apollo space ship about to take off
any minute/ that's exactly what happened at the stonewall/

MILES: you were at stonewall?

BILLY: she was one of the original gals/ friday night june 27th,
1969, there was this full hot moon & any faggot in town knew that
the stonewall was the spot to check/ Francine was there, as gay as
all the daisies she wore in her hair/ the afro was then her political
statement/

(actual footage of the stonewall riots is shown)

FRANCINE: by midnight, the joint got jammed packed/ everybody
jacked up on jolly beans/ SLY & THE FAMILY STONE kept singing:
"wanna take you higher!" all queens screamed higher, getting the
spirit from that record when the 6th precinct cops busted in/ they
booked all the employees/ one by one, they let us out/ i was waiting
with bambi for china doll who was still inside when this paddy wagon
arrived/ catcalls & boos went wild/ this hot spanish boy yelled: "yo
soy maricon y me gusta/ venceremos hermanos y hermanas/ let's turn
this muthafuckah ovah"/ we would have too if it didn't drive away full
steamed/ most them white queens were just bitching on the side-
walks, fixing their long hair, trying to make up their mind on where
else to party but we black girls had been through that shit in civil
rights demonstrations/ we knew that stonewall was mostly a white
joint but that was our place to party/ we couldn't take no more/ i
mean we wouldn't take no more/ we were READDDY/ china doll held a
show, putting up some fight with 2 cops who escorted her out, kicking

& yelling: "get your claws off my titties, pig!" she got an ovation/ bambi screamed: "give it to them sister/ tell it like it is"/ i heard a bottle crash against the brick wall/ then another/ this cop shouted he'd been hurt/ cans started flying out of nowhere/ wigs flipped/ windows smashed/ police cars sirened by sheridan square when some of the white girls joined us & got physical/ next thing i knew, i was in the middle of this full-blown riot/ i saw this big black cop coming at me, mad & vicious like some bleeding bull/ "how can he do this?" i heard bambi say but then i was so furious, i lifted this uprooted parking meter with all the strength i could muster/ i was hercules & i threw it at him with all my rage/ it crashed against the door just as i felt something hot, something hard hit the back of my neck, once, twice, three times, fast/

(FRANCINE lays on stage)

BILLY: she passed out/ that was the start of her career of confrontations with cops/

(the SPIRIT brings the guitar to FRANCINE/ as the latter plays & sings, the SPIRIT plants on stage picket signs on which the grievances of gay people are written)

FRANCINE: I AM DONE WITH CRAWLING
I CAN'T LIVE ON A STRING
ALL I WANT IS OUR DREAM
THE AMERICAN DREAM
WE WERE TOLD COULD BE TRUE
WE HAVE LOST ME & YOU
I WISH INDEED WE COULD BE
RISIN' TO THE LOVE WE NEED

I BEEN SO DOWN
YEAH WAY WAY DOWN

BUT NOW I'M UP
I'M GONNA GET TO THE TOP
WITH ALL THE FAITH IN MY HEART
NOW THAT I KNOW WHERE TO START
I FEEL INDEED I WILL BE
RISIN' TO THE LOVE WE NEED

I AM BLACK & I AM GAY
I'M HAPPY THAT WAY
I'M HERE, HERE TO STAY
I WON'T CRY & I WON'T PRAY
I'M READY TO PLAY
PLAY WITH YOU, PLAY AWAY
I KNOW INDEED WE WILL BE
RISIN' TO THE LOVE WE NEED

MILES: indian summer 1979 was on time/ i didn't last no time at all but i was risin' to the love we need/

SUNNI: (*coming out of the piers*) that bitch making another speech?

FRANCINE: Sunni, why don't you join us?

SUNNI: please/ a bunch of bourgeois black queens acting like it was the last scene/

(*calling someone who's still inside the piers*)

sweetiepie, are you coming?

(*a gorgeous black guy steps out/ SUNNI puts his arm around him & turns on his cassette player full volume to "Good Times" by CHIC*)

i'se gonna get mucho mocca chocolata tonite/ lady & gentle queens . . .

(to ASSOTTO)

douche

(to FRANCINE)

gargle

(to BILLY)

& be sweet/

(to MILES)

black beauty, you better find yourself a home tonight/

(SUNNI & the gorgeous stranger exit)

MILES: the first two weeks, he brought roses/ the third, a piggy bank with 3 pennies/ one for health, one for love, one for happiness/ each time he'd visit, i'd fix tails, feet, snouts, rice & beans, corn bread, carrot cake & all these nice things a black queen does to keep her cat pleased/

FRANCINE: child, where on earth did you pick up this prince charming?

MILES: he hired me for this office job/

FRANCINE: he was your boss too?

MILES: *(shakes his head)* the first day, i saw that wedding ring/

(negative reaction from FRANCINE& BILLY)

bobby was very serious about divorce/ his wife got vicious when she found out/ said crazy things like if he left her, she'd never let him come close to junior/ he loved that kid & he loved this one here too/

(slides depicting the following scenes are projected)

one sunday afternoon, the three of us picnicked in the park/ i watched that little boy, bouncing & laughing on his daddy's shoulders/ next morning, i called in my resignation/ that night, bobby rushed to my place but i, my own judas christ kissed him, sent him home to his kid forever/ all i'm left with are memories & these three pennies/

FRANCINE: *(comforts a sobbing MILES)* child, this upset ritual's nothing but an emotional test in your survival kit/

BILLY: come on, too many tears will kill you/ what will happen when all that water runs out?

FRANCINE: he's young/ he's strong/ he'll get along/

BILLY: waiting/ waiting/ the hurt is not only when you're left but when you're out here, searching, waiting/

(walks downstage)

when i pass by you, don't just look at my fine face, my nice tight ass or my hard-on/ see the heart beneath the skin/ reach for it/ it's my gift/

(MILES whispers into FRANCINE's ears/ she takes her guitar & accompanies MILES as he walks to BILLY & sings)

MILES: SHOW ME A PLACE WHERE THE SUN SHINES ETERNALLY
SHOW ME THE SUMMER, SHOW ME THE LAUGHTER

SHOW ME A PLACE THAT'S FROM HERE TO ETERNITY
SHOW ME THE WONDERS, WONDERS OF YOUR HEART

SHOW ME, SHOW ME, SHOW ME, SHOW ME, SHOW ME TO YOUR
HEART BABY
THAT'S WHERE I WANT TO BE
SHOW ME, SHOW ME, SHOW ME, SHOW ME, SHOW ME TO YOUR
HEART BABY
FOREVER

BILLY: (*sings to MILES*) SHOW ME DESIRE, DESIRE IN ALL ITS FORMS
SHOW ME THE RAPTURE, SHOW ME THE FUTURE
SHOW ME DESIRE, DESIRE AS STRONG AS STORMS
SHOW ME THE FIRES, FIRES OF YOUR HEART

BILLY & MILES: SHOW ME, SHOW ME, SHOW ME, SHOW ME,
SHOW ME TO YOUR HEART BABY
THAT'S WHERE I WANT TO BE
SHOW ME, SHOW ME, SHOW ME, SHOW ME, SHOW ME TO YOUR
HEART BABY
THAT'S WHERE I GOT TO BE
FOREVER

(they hesitate then kiss/ MILES tosses the three pennies to the
SPIRIT/ FRANCINE embraces both/ ASSOTTO, who had been observ-
ing all this & been moved, joins them)

ASSOTTO: i'm standing here angry, the bitterness has been there
so long, eating me like cancer/ i could shelter in my hurt but i don't
wish to live a dead life/ i want to transcend this black gay label
which often cut through the madness, yet stops short of the needs/
when i face myself in a mirror, i'll never mistake who i see/ not this
fantasy of what i should be/ not a parody of the person i could be/
my aliveness is in my willingness to be all that's me/

(walks downstage)

father, happiness wherever you may be/ out of the grubs covering
your heart, may a rose sprout/

*(FRANCINE gathers MILES, ASSOTTO & BILLY around her as she
unpins the four gardenias in her hairdo, she says)*

FRANCINE: we have come of age in a world that has come of age for us/

*(the SPIRIT unties the bandanna around her head, the bandanna
containing ASSOTTO's burnt dreams, wrings drops of sweat & ash
on each gardenia then exits/ FRANCINE pins a flower on MILES,
BILLY, ASSOTTO & herself)*

ever since i saw pictures of josephine baker in feathers & them foot-
high head-dresses, knew that's what i wanted to be/ dreamed i'd
sing & dance on broadway/

*(slides depicting the various scenes are used throughout
the next sketch)*

when i was fifteen, growing up as franklin delano robinson in mont-
gomery, alabama with mama, daddy & all my five sisters, i paid
no mind to how cruel neighbors could get about my cross-dressing
'cause my folks just let me be/ that was 1955, the year grand-ma
died/ grand-ma who always told us to walk with our heads high/ '55,
the year rosa parks refused to move to the back of bus/ on christmas
day, i came across this picture of josephine & her rainbow tribe/ i
remember i thought how great it was for a black woman who grew
up in st. louis, missouri, amidst all kinds of racial upheavals, to
overcome all those superficial obstacles in our lives & set out to
achieve her dream of universal brotherhood/ i looked at those little
kids' colorful faces, the difference yet the loving/ i clipped that

picture out of the paper/ each night, i would place it under my pillow & i'd hear good soulful music flow/ music which eased my mind/
music that made me dream/

january 1st, 1956, i stole fifty bucks from my older sister's piggy
bank/ money betty lou had been saving to get her wedding dress in
june/ early that morning, i packed my bags, got on the next train to
detroit, michigan/ i was heading north to do my thing/ got started in
this little downtown joint where everybody had been in the life/ for
thirteen years, i dragged my act all over cleveland, ohio . . . detroit,
michigan . . . baltimore, maryland . . . chicago, illinois . . . philadelphia, pa . . .& in april 1969, new york city where i've been paying my
dues/ lately, dreaming some handsome humpy dude will come along
with lots of love & lots of dough & i'd retire to a nice domestic life
upstate, possibly jersey with two foster kids & my man/

november 7th 1976, i attended this special tribute to josephine at
lincoln center, like so many of us who loved her & believed her cause
didn't die back in april 1975/ for an entire month, i turned tricks,
morning, noon & night so i could get me this superb white satin
sequined dress i'd seen in a bloomingdale's window/ i must say, i
looked as dignified as princess grace & glamorous like jackie o/ that
night, i took the a train back to harlem/ soon as i laid my head on the
mattress, josephine appeared to me & she said

SPIRIT: (*dressed a la josephine*) the rainbow tribe touches on what
may be the most vital question human beings face: how to deal with
each other/ i've been quite worried that no one is assuming leadership of my mission & i hope in years to come, my children will rep-
resent every point of view as well as all colors & religions because
that is where true freedom lies/ Francine, you are my child too & i
hope you won't let me down/ the rainbow tribe has advanced us all a
thousand years/

ASSOTTO: since 1976, each new year's eve, Francine started lighting a candle to mark what she considered the most historical event that happened the past year in the progress for better human relations/ on july 4th, she had watched the tall ships sail into the hudson from all over the world, the spectacular fireworks that night in the harbor, the statue of liberty beaming with light/ more than ever, she believed in her country/ 200 years was just the beginning because there's no limit to where we're heading/

FRANCINE: & i lighted a candle/

(the SPIRIT lights a candle on stage)

ASSOTTO: in 1977, she hailed anwar sadat for his pilgrimage to jerusalem which she saw as the biggest momentum for peace in the middle east/ blessed are the peace-makers, read the cards she sent to both him & begin/

FRANCINE: & i lighted a candle/

(the SPIRIT lights a candle on stage)

ASSOTTO: in '78 she watched, as millions of us, the absolute stillness at jonestown/ what religious fervor & misplaced faith could do/ that she took as a lesson from which we could all learn, specially with the born-again movement sweeping the country/ that year, she cried bitterly when harvey milk was murdered/

FRANCINE: still, i lighted a candle/

(the SPIRIT lights another candle/ slides of watergate, vietnam, discos are shown/ actual footage of the march on washington should be used)

in '79, i celebrated coping with the ropes of the me decade/ the third-world gay conference & the march/ october 14, washington d.c., when i got off the disco train, i kissed the ground like john paul the second/ i jumped like a holy roller on capitol hill when i saw thousands & thousands of gay folks, three-hundred thousand strong/ i blew kisses to the third-world sisters heading the parade but all love few out of my heart to the biggest group honey, from new york city/ i shouted whoopee when this lesbian said loud for all the nation to hear: "if freedom shall ring in this country, let it ring for all americans or in time, it shall not ring at all!" & i lighted a candle/

(the SPIRIT lights another candle)

i've been feeling so apart from everybody/ at times, so removed from reality & i am after that which is beyond what i got now/ not just a statement either/ that picture of josephine which i still place under my pillow, the songs, lighting candles, the march today & in the future, all that ain't enough/ i know where i'm coming from better than ever/ i don't know where i'm heading but i'm willing for all of us blacks, gays, bis, tvs, etc etc, all of us who are holding on to this american dream, all of us who are withholding peace, to give each other love & respect: the gifts of the magi/ right now, right here, from a brand-new beginning, mold america; america, not yet land of the free but for sure, home of the brave/ tonight, i have screamed out pain/ i have screamed out frustration/ what was so horrible can pass & i won't accept that which is horrible/ i can understand slavery/ i can understand homophobia/ i can understand sexism & i can understand racism/ it's all a big misunderstanding/ a holding back & there's ecstasy in the sharing/ i tell you, sheer ecstasy in sharing/ america's already so divided, so disembodied that if we keep ghettoizing ourselves, it leads us to more wars/ like this crumbling pier, leaves us in ruins/

BILLY: Francine, you are one queen with a whole lotta loving/ your life's all in your dreams & your dreams are all your life/

MILES: good god! when i see somebody who can survive the slumps like she did, it just fascinates me/

FRANCINE: so often, i have made promises to myself, i could recite them all/ whatever the toughness, i will not live blind to my own needs & my needs are coming up/ like king kong, honey, they are coming up/

(the SPIRIT unfolds her cape, lifting her arms high above her head, looking like a rainbow)

i am not going to be upheld for a freak anymore & i should not be here, screaming out my values when they happen to be human values/ so what are you going to do with all this loving energy? i ain't looking at nobody else but you/

(she sings a cappella)

I AM READY, DO YOU HEAR ME
ARE YOU READY, WILL YOU PLEASE ME

(the SPIRIT writes in the clouds in neon light the phrase RISIN' TO THE LOVE WE NEED as the others join FRANCINE in singing)

RISIN' TO THE LOVE WE NEED
RISIN' TO THE LOVE WE NEED
RISIN' TO THE LOVE WE NEED

END

Black Fag
(a performance art piece in 4 parts)

"one's outer life passes in a solitude haunted by the masks of others; one's inner life passes in a solitude haunted by the masks of one's self."

—Eugene O'Neill

"sweetheart, your bathroom is the only place where one time or another, you got to strip yourself naked!"

—Counsel Wright

the performer, the voice on the vocoder & the audience/

a bathroom: a sink, a tub, a bowl, a mirror hanging above the sink, a hamper, a record player & a screen that drops at the beginning of each part on which titles & credits are flashed/ they're all surrounded by a white fence/

23 masks, each revealing a different facet of the performer's personality & also different masks for the audience/

hello wonderland: a round painting, childlike, simple, consisting of a mountain of black brushstrokes & out of the mountaintop rises a sun giving off bright colored rays/ in the sky area of the painting, these words from genesis are printed: "IN THE BEGINNING GOD CREATED THE HEAVENS & THE EARTH WAS WITHOUT FORM & VOID & THE DARK-NESS WAS UPON THE FACE OF THE EARTH & THE SPIRIT OF GOD MOVED UPON THE FACE OF THE WATERS & GOD SAID LET THERE BE LIGHT & THERE WAS LIGHT"/

cruising costume: black patrick sneakers, 501 levi's & ripped t-shirt/ a dancer's black brief that the performer wears from the beginning/ different detergent boxes/

1) *hallow we're in: faces of fear/ 6:00 p.m.*
2) *mineshaft/ midnight*
3) *hello wonderland/ 6:00 a.m.*
4) *eternity's children/ noon*

HALLOW WE'RE IN: FACES OF FEAR

(no curtain/ the performer is sleeping in his briefs, in the middle of the stage as the spectators come in/ each spectator is given a mask which he or she is instructed to wear during the ritual/ if no one wishes to wear a mask, let a dummy be used/ we hear an alarm clock ring/ the performer wakes up, grouchy & walks over to the record player/ he turns it on/ while the record "FACES OF FEAR" plays, the performer brushes his teeth & washes his face/ on the screen, like in movies, a list of credits is flashed, e.g. actor's name, director's, etc., then in bold caption "HALLOW WE'RE IN: FACES OF FEAR"; NEW YORK CITY, OCTOBER 31, 6:00 P.M./ the performer speaks over the music as he raises his face to look at himself in the mirror)

after each time i wash up
i fantasize about which one of my *many faces*
i will be seen in/

(walks over to the record player & picks up the record)

watch out, sybil darling
this sister is going to be

(smashes the record on the floor)

the record-breaking queen/

(indicating the various masks that hang on the mirror)

count them all
twenty-three & coming up with brand-new ones
you ain't seen yet/

274

(takes down a mask, puts it on & acts the part)
i can be all slicked-up jerry curls
shades pulled down
walking real heavy
acting like any bourgeois niggah dressed right out of ebony/

(takes off the mask, takes down another & acts the part)

this is how i look on monday mornings
listening to the news which do nothing
but present me with pressure
trying to trace myself in a calendar
because when i leave the office on friday afternoons
i clock the world out of my mind/
ain't got responsibility to nobody except be happy/
you see, the powers that be are going to blow
this whole planet off the face of the universe
including me, that's *destiny*/
by the end of the century, a fait accompli/
at least if they do it on a weekend
i'll go on a slightly highhhhhher level
know what i mean/

(takes off the mask, takes down another & acts the part)

many of you have seen the carefree me
footloose like a true sissy on a disco floor/
ouh ouh ouh ouh . . . ouh ouh ouh . . . please don't step on my corns
i'll whizz by you
easy like the summer breeze/

(takes off the mask, takes down another & acts the part)

this one here ranks as my all-time favorite

poor little me, sitting in a bar
looking like bette after she done lost one of her lovers/
eyes of pretty promises
sipping the anxiety/

(takes off the mask)

besides, liquor & tissues cost a pretty penny/
let me open my nut-bag & bring out . . .

(opens the hamper & takes out his cruising mask & attire, which he
puts on as he describes them)

my black patrick sneakers
these 501 levi's & ripped t-shirt that help express best my figure
i'm going to be mother vampire & hit the streets
head crowned tight with a red rag
padded with this 9-inch ad/

(pressing his penis)

have you ever seen a bitch without her tail?
ain't nothing new!

(opens the fence door & walks offstage)

i've been out here for trouble & survival
since i started making the scene at sixteen/

(strolls amidst the audience)

do you feel i'm putting on an act for you?
well . . .
what would you like me to do with something that's first nature

276

something that all of us find so real
somehow we can't quite kill . . . houh . . .

(strolls amidst the audience, admiring their masks)

actually, halloween is small-time treat
compared to the nightly eerie reality of christopher street/
i don't get why we gays fuss much over it/
same old pick your prick trick & treat that started on day one/
if i may say, some of us look like we've been here
since the day after/
i guess, one night a year we got to pretend
that's not how we come on to each other/
all this is just a put-on . . .
or maybe it's the night of realization
that we've been masked all along
so we hide behind faked ones
remaining faces of *fear*

*(keeps walking amidst the audience as if in a trance, examining
them for the first time)*

faces of fear
faces of fear
faces of fear
faces of fear
faces of fear
faces of fear
forever faces of fear in a hallow we're in . . .

*(for two minutes or so, he goes into a self-observation, watching
everything that goes on around him & watching himself/ it's also a
fear process)*

here i am with a thousand shadows of myself
looking for the next smoke
applying needles to open up
dropping the alcohol
playing all kinds of jungle games to survive
each one of us carrying on his own war
so guarded we don't know what we're guarding
never cutting through the madness/
long ago, i lost track whether i'm coming
going
in between
or just having one bad dream/
& i thought this was the real thing/
can't breathe . . . .
been shrinking inside . . .
ain't got guts to touch the lifenessness in my life/

(he bends down & picks up dirt from the floor & rubs it on his face)

i'm going to scratch off my reality these fucked-up fantasies that do
me in 'stead of lead the real me out . . .

(he scratches harder & harder)

out . . .
out . . .

*(he scratches desperately for two minutes or so, removing the cruis-
ing mask to reveal another)*

like some ghost catching hell
i am crazed with pain/

(starts a rain dance)

got to dance

        dance

            dance

                dance for the rain . . .

    (dances crazier & crazier back to the stage/ fade out)

MINESHAFT

(spotlight on bathtub where the performer bathes, suds covering his entire body/ he is staring at a white mask on the wall/he's totally transfixed/ on the screen is projected the title: "MINE-SHAFT: MIDNIGHT")

from childhood
i carried my blackness as a cross/
knocked out
white nails/

(he gets up & takes down the mask, examines it, reliving a memory)

i am done though
done with hunting after white guys to raise me high . . .
done with easing good through many of the wild fantasies . . .
done with the bitter silence that gnaws like cancer . . .
last night

        (looking back at the tub)

in that tub at the mineshaft
bare
i stared
beyond the still thick smoke
beyond the bulged crotches

beyond the milling flies
beyond the blessed beauties: statues posed against the walls
beyond those boys bent for joy
beyond the dreams of bathing in a thousand white dudes' cum
to wash a dark shade off my skin
beyond the dreams of their fingers grasping my head still
to wave the wooliness out of my hair
beyond the dreams of their golden showers
a' falling
a' streaming hot over my face
to melt the imperfect
beyond . . .
beyond . . .
i shut my eyes for an instant
to forget the hurt
in never loved
been loved as i needed/

(he cracks the mask in his hands & drops the pieces in the tub)

i screamed
ran out to the piers like a mad man
my big uncut dick beating beep beep beep 'gainst my belly
reaching for the horizon/
deep into the hudson i plunged
sailed on a thousand waves
to the rhythm of twenty million blackhearts' beat
aspired
my arms full with the soft sun
demystified . . .

(he gets sick & runs to the bowl, where he vomits)

(fade out)

HELLO WONDERLAND

(we hear the sound of a toilet flushing/ spotlight on the performer,
vomiting into the bowl/ feeling better, he raises his face/ on the
screen is flashed the title: HELLO WONDERLAND: 6:00 A.M.)

when i was 9
a smile
a kind word were my winning numbers/
i wanted to be a priest/
there was something about christ & the gift of the magi
i thought had to be delivered more to the universe/
i also wanted to be an artist/
i got holy magic out of mixing colors
that spell-bound me for hours/
the earth was wonderland/
wonderland was a rainbow in my child's mind/

(sits on the toilet bowl)

as i got older
discovered
trusted all my black gay elements
i found out about labels/
paid the price . . .
when even the church i counted on had no place for me
i wrecked the altar i'd built in my bedroom
cut the lillies & daisies
burned all the saints's pictures
& deep in my backyard, buried the statue of jesus of prague/
a statue i had adored/
for the next sixteen years i locked myself inside my gayness
where i felt safest

lately tried desperately to lead a carefree life
letting my mind be preoccupied with the dollar
& surviving sexual services/
i am a product of america/
i scratched my ass & got glad with the 9 to 5/
but coming home after tripping all night long

as i closed my eyes
i heard screaming fetuses plucked out of wombs
i heard a billion hungry babies' bellies growl
i heard a.i.d.s who will be next . . . a.i.d.s. who will be next . . .
i heard america
england
                              russia
                                    france
                                          china
                                          & india racing
arms in arms

i heard sixty megaton bombs ticking a requiem for new york city
i heard grenades in el salvador
popping like firecrackers on july fourth
i heard the firing squad in iran
i heard palestine's dreams blown up
i heard zimbabwe's moans & groans
i heard haitians yearning to breathe
i heard crosses crackle in ireland
i heard swastikas being planted on lawns
i just can't take one more moonie with plastic smile
selling me roses that don't smell
i can't take the pope kissing the ground where
jerry falwell stomps & waves the bible like a weapon
i can't take the city council voting down my civil rights
i hear all this shit that ain't music

i get sick & can't sleep easy/
the nightmare life has become so much too brutal
that i lock myself in this bathroom/
i can't help but fall inside the tears/

(he vomits into the bowl/ after a while, we hear a vocoder voice
chant the following: "IN THE BEGINNING, GOD CREATED THE
HEAVENS & THE EARTH & THE EARTH WAS WITHOUT FORM &
VOID & THE DARKNESS WAS UPON THE FACE OF THE EARTH & THE
SPIRIT OF GOD MOVED UPON THE FACE OF THE WATERS & GOD
SAID LET THERE BE LIGHT & THERE WAS LIGHT"/ the performer
raises his face out of the bowl as if recognizing the voice)

i remember when i first read those words
child of nine that i was
i sought in my own fashion to manifest my feelings
for the beauty of creation/

(he gets up & swings the mirror to reveal a painting)

"WONDERLAND!" my first painting
my first painting which survived the turbulence of the angry years
my first painting which survived because there's an innocence
to be treasured like stuffs dreams are made of/

(he takes down the painting & tears it apart then throws the pieces
at the audience/ he keeps the frame)

i release it to you like birds
i release it to you like birds in the sky/
from now on, i shall carry this empty frame to every street corner
so we may see what we have done
how empty we've become . . .
beyond the labels

(he finally removes the final mask to reveal his naked face)

beyond the masks
beyond the costumes
beyond the stage

(he walks offstage with the frame)

beyond the performances
in an act of love we could come together
naked
& recreate piece by piece our WONDERLAND!

(walks amidst the audience, holding the frame as he sings)

hello, you out there
how do you do/
hello, what has happened to me & you/
hello, do you care
for something new/
hello, what has our world been coming to/

don't you see the nukes they plant at our doors
don't you smell the fish that rot on our shores
don't you hear the leaves that fall from our trees
don't you eat that crap they sell in our stores
don't you feel our bodies' unhealing sores
don't you hear these pleas that burst out of me/

hello, you out there
wake up & stand/
hello, when will we bring this waste to end/
hello, do you care to lend a hand/
hello, let's build again our wonderland . . .

let's build again our wonderland . . .
let's build again our wonderland . . .

(then he says)

4 billion birds flocking together with all their songs
such a colorful canvas . . .
ouh . . . what a winning that would be/

(fade out)

ETERNITY'S CHILDREN

*(the performer is on his knees, scrubbing the floor with his clothes,
surrounded by detergent boxes & bottles/ he's humming "Hello
Wonderland"/ he interacts with the audience that surrounds him/
on the screen the title "ETERNITY'S CHILDREN: HIGH NOON" is
projected)*

not much prettiness left to this earth except for flowers
a flock of birds flying far into the sunset
these wide-open skies at sunrise
with the mist rolling just above the hudson
so i can't see the dirt/
not much prettiness left
& if times square here is an example of america the beautiful
baby we sure got a long way to go/
folks be looking clean
smelling clean
& acting like dogs/
no hint of humanity/
that's the life i lived & leaving behind/

(pours more detergent on the floor)

when i told my mother about my future plans
the woman snapped out/
kept waving her ten fingers in my face
hollering she'd pay for a shrink or a caribbean vacation/
later for her/
my darling, darling friends all said
"don't worry 'bout politics!
whatever will be shall be/
ain't nothing you can do 'bout it/
honey, take some acid & have a good trip/
relax . . . besides, you're not even a citizen/ "
i pay taxes, don't i?
i won't eat shit sandwiches from these bullshitters
we've allowed to be our visionaries/
you got people walking around
who don't believe indians were slaughtered
or they write books & make movies about
happy-go-lucky gigging giggling slaves/
they'll sleep through their own demise & reincarnation/
i've been through hell & i'm just coming back
can't even explain to you the spiritual high i had
the minute i went down on my knees
started scrubbing/
words fail me/
nowadays i gain weight on pure contentment
but it's too heavy for most folks to deal with
because that's reality
a new dimension of me/

(pointing to an imaginary figure nearby)

check out that jackass walking into the wall
'cause he don't dare look at me/
watch them hurry by

286

trying to think i'm not here doing what i'm doing/
with all that extra effort not to acknowledge me
they're just adding trash on their eyelids
feathers to my cap
earlier this afternoon, a punk-rocker passed me by
a swastika on his armband/
i was getting ready to go after him
when i realized the kid's probably more scared than i am
& i too am caught up on all this fear
because i'm caught up on america
america . . . 200 million fucked-up attitudes clashing together
& that becomes "GOOD EVENING,
THIS IS THE NIGHTLY NEWS:"
the stuff you read in history books
the stuff of nightmares
the stuff of our puffed-ball mentality lives
& that's the way it is, day in day out/
revelations winding down much too quick
you know it's the last book/
oh! i waited so long for this miracle/
all i want now is the strength to do what's got to be done/

(gathering all the detergent boxes & bottle & the pot with water)

it's the ingredients that make the output
& i was born for outdoor cleanliness & indoor happiness/
got me this *fab* idea

(takes hold of a spectator's feet & removes the shoes & socks then
pours some fab detergent on the bare feet)

got me this *fab* idea

(pours some dash detergent on the feet & scrubs them)

287

& just one little *dash* of this *fab* idea of mine

        (pours fresh start detergent)

gonna wash you up & give you a *fresh start*

        (pours some wisk detergent)

wisk you *all*

        (pours dawn & era detergent)

wisk you *all* into the *dawn* of a new *era*

        (pours joy & cheer detergent)

an *era* of *joy & cheer* yeah . . .

        (pours sunlight detergent)

gonna see the *sunlight*

        (pours yes detergent)

you'll scream *yes yes yes* more & more

        (pours solo & dynamo detergent)

because you never felt that *solo dynamo* before/

        (pours some bold detergent)

you gonna be *bold*

(pours final touch detergent)

for the *final touch*

(he wipes the feet with cling-free sheets)

you'll *cling free*/
you hear, you'll cling free/
now i know i'm a pussy & fussy black fag
but if i don't wash you up
you & i will have nothing in common/
you might bypass what i'm doing
after this moment, there'll be an understanding of it all/
time's a factor!
our world is in desperate need of bold folks to apply their minds
& connect their understanding with their guts/
can you imagine how many planets we could join
if we were metaphysically clean/
if we put to proper use what we got
no other living species on this earth ain't got/
a wonderous mind/
if instead of extincting ourselves, we extended ourselves

(he removes the mask of the spectator whose feet he has just washed, kisses him or her on the forehead then hands detergent & towels to that spectator & signals for him or her to wash the next spectator's feet & so on . . .)

beyond . . .
beyond . . .
beyond . . .
beyond . . .

(scrubbing the floor, the air, everything that's around him)

all my life, i have been on a roller-coaster ride of drives
to nowhere
twirling with my colorful shadows
each time the heart got too hot
each time the soul got too soft/
but today, i anchored full-stop
to deliver to the universe my testimony
which might be my ass's first touch with reality/
if you aren't ready to deal with it
mail it back to the wind
uncensored/
i'll be waiting
biding for time
& i'm scratching ETERNITY . . .

(on the screen is flashed the sentence "& THE SAGA CONTINUES . . .")

New Love Song
[a multimedia theater piece]

THE TIME

july 4th, 1986/ statue of liberty centennial/ new york city/

THE CHARACTERS

SKY: *the singer/ 39 years old/ black/ he wears a white robe embroidered with glass beads, doves, birds & butterflies, sylphs & rainbows/*

ROCK: *the sculptor/ 50 years old/ black/ he wears a green robe embroidered with leather leaves, trees, flowers & gnomes/*

NILE: *the dancer/ 19 years old/ black/ he wears a blue robe embroidered with tortoise shells, fish, sirens, yemanja & undines*

BLAISE: *the writer/ 28 years old/ black/ he wears a red robe embroidered with lizard skin, sun, satellites, volcanoes, & salamanders/ in one scene, he wears a grace jones drag/*

THE SET

part-temple cum sanctuary, part-gallery cum performance space/

TO THE DIRECTOR

dare to be more/ the piece is a ritual therefore stylization & a formal atmosphere are becoming/ masks & robes should be used/ (darkness/ a silent film is projected, showing various events commemorating the july 4th, 1986, statue of liberty centennial in new york city: tall ships, parades, crowds, bands, speeches, battery park/ downstage left, sky views the film & sings)

SKY: I HAVE LOST TRACK, FACING THIS NOTHINGNESS ALL DAY
INSPIRATIONS, THERE ARE NO CREATIONS
HERE I AM TRAPPED WITH DREAMS THAT DIED ALONG THE WAY
I ONLY KNOW I CANNOT GO ON
UNEASY WITH MYSELF

MADNESS IS IT MADNESS I'M COMING TO
MADNESS IS IT MADNESS I'M GOING THROUGH
WHO AM I
WHY AM I
UNEASY WITH MYSELF

SO MANY THOUGHTS TOSSING & TURNING IN MY HEAD
ALL QUESTIONS WHERE ARE THE SOLUTIONS
BIDING MY TIME & PLAYING SILLY GAMES INSTEAD
I ONLY KNOW I CANNOT GO ON
UNEASY WITH MYSELF

MADNESS IS IT MADNESS I'M COMING TO
MADNESS IS IT MADNESS I'M GOING THROUGH
WHO AM I
WHY AM I
UNEASY WITH MYSELF

MADNESS IS IT MADNESS I'M COMING TO
MADNESS IS IT MADNESS I'M GOING THROUGH
WHO AM I
WHY AM I
UNEASY WITH MYSELF

*(as the song peaks, we hear howling winds/eerie wails/ unearthly
moans/ cries & whispers/ nerve-rending screams/ sky walks into the
shadows, center stage/ in front of fluttering curtains, he kneels on
the bare earth stage, beside nile, rock & blaise/ they are celebrants*

conjuring a different new world through chant/ sky: air element,
faces east/ nile: water element, faces west/ rock: earth element,
faces north/ blaise: fire element, faces south)

SKY, NILE, ROCK & BLAISE: I REMEMBER THE BEGINNING
A DREAM ANCIENT AS DAWN
A DREAM OF DESTINY DRUMMING UP
THE BLOOD
OUR FLESH
THIS EARTH
A DREAM WE WERE ONCE ONE
SOUL

(we hear the jingle of a miniature carousel revolving above cen-
ter stage as the fluttering curtains are drawn to reveal a dimly lit
spacious garden of magnificent monuments & barbaric statues of
bronze & painted welded steel, rock paintings, mobiles & tapes-
try, african masks & sacred artifacts such as clay pots, pitchers &
fetishes/ framed pictures of icons of black gays abound e.g.
sylvester, diana ross, patti labelle, ntozake shange, martin luther
king/ here & there, a few ceremonial stools/ the back wall is a
mural illuminated with colorful hieroglyphs/ up center stage, with
a united states of america flag flying on top of it, a pine tree rises:
tall, evergreen, life-affirming, axis mundi/
part-temple cum sanctuary, part-gallery cum performance space,
the architecture provides the poetical background for the ritual that
will take place/
follow-up spotlight picks up sky, master of the spirits as he guides
the elements on this journey to discover cosmic truths for them-
selves as black gay people)

SKY: in america
where omens abound out of control
i often come to this garden

sing swing high
sing swing right to the sky each time i sing
i give bodies to my dreams

ROCK: half-lives
who on the brink of a new breath
kept shrinking

SKY: i give faces to my fantasies

NILE: which allowed themselves to be
shadows
dancing into their own graves

SKY: i give voices to my memories

BLAISE: desperate to bear witness
& settle accounts
choking on silence

SKY: i give a heart to my needs

ROCK: testing time
testing strength

BLAISE: haunted by the future

NILE: no longer abiding
by the 20th century

    (the jingle of the carousel fades out as the lights brighten)

SKY: i have sheltered these black gay elements
deep in my soul

this july 4th, 1986
they thrive
in my new love song

(there's an abrupt light change which shocks rock, nile & blaise/ they
scream & shout in frenzy)

ROCK, NILE & BLAISE: faggots . . .
niggahs . . .

SKY: a label can denigrate you
a label can make you hate yourself

(assuming a collective bigoted attitude, nile, rock & blaise march
onstage with banners & posters that read: "sodomy is an un-amer-
ican activity/ ship all them lazy bastard niggahs back to africa/ kill
all these faggot disease carriers/ long live the kkk, united states of
america & god" making great noise & causing upheaval throughout
sky's speech)

images limited in scope
yet so often floated
they blocked my vision of reality
still caught up in a time which steals
away time
we closet ourselves
or criticize america
to be nothing
but a baseball-addicted country
of beer-bellied bigots & idiots
i ain't quite comfortable
with my own stereotypes
(sky gestures for the others to discard banners & posters so they may
return to their collective black gay identity)

in my world of worlds
every citizen sees
himself
a masterpiece
yet a simple american

(sky gestures to blaise as if inviting him to speak or recite a poem)

BLAISE: one night
lost outside myself
elements scattered
i searched
for a testimony to 28 years
for a testament to those i kept loving
for self-singularity to some social security number
i found poems i had discarded
read them
the miracle that moment worked up my guts
to hold out tripping into oblivion
on my resume write survivor
better yet i'll write it myself
not just black on white printed words
which don't mean a thing to non-english speaking folks
but my story

(the others respond with their own anecdotes which form a collec-
tive black gay identity)

NILE: filled with bare calloused corned feet
beat the earth mercilessly
each time the rhythm gets too funky
BLAISE: filled with tree-trunk thighs
torched crotch

SKY: filled with foreign intrigue
ancestral spirits

BLAISE: filled with visions of harvey's & martin's dreams

SKY: filled with myths not yet sung

BLAISE: i am writing my story
natural & free
self-pity can't possibly be part of my vocabulary
like mount st helen erupting in glory

SKY, NILE, ROCK & BLAISE: AMERICA
WE ARE BORN AGAIN
IN THE FULL SUNLIGHT
WE LIFT OUR HEADS SKY HIGH
SING OUT OUR MESSAGES

(blaise & sky exit/ nile enacts & dances the following story which rock narrates)

ROCK: last july 4th, like every july 4th for four years, nile ground
ginger roots & lime rind, spooned brown sugar in a cup of cock-spur
ram he gulped/ carrying on his head
all the front pages
of new york post for the past year
all the front pages
with sorry stories
all the front pages
with mad headlines
which had struck & hurt his eyes, he climbed the stairs of his
abandoned building on eighth street between b&c/ in the center of
the cement rooftop, he heaped the papers on which he gracefully

stripped/ he rubbed greek-imported olive oil over his body to catch
more heat/
staring straight at the sun
nile waited to hear the voice
staring straight at the sun
nile waited to feel the beat
staring straight at the sun
nile waited till his teeth clacked
with a shriek so hot it set the heap on fire, round & round the flames
he ran, talking in tongues then, on the roof's edge, he perched in
arabesque, like an eagle ready for flight/ high above his head, he
lifted his arms/ in his fluttering fingers, the sun shattered/ the universe stood still while nile smiled/ an empowering mystery, the past
passed on from generations, all the joy of life reflected/ so slowly,
his body bent far forward/ long supple arms opened low
to pay homage
to surrender in prayer
to offer himself

     a black queen   dancing with shadows
             at high noon
triple trouble that's brutal

NILE: (*as he exits*) chasing america's evil spirits away
               away
                     away

*(nile enters followed by rock/ blaise enters & picks up a copy of the
book For Colored Girls . . . & he addresses the picture of ntozake
shange on the cover)*

BLAISE: ntozake shange
i looked you up
among the poets at barnes & noble
but i didn't find you

walt was there amidst leaves of grass
anne gazed down
glazed eyes dreamt of rowing & mercy
erica posed in her latest erotica
even rod took much space
i searched among ghosts
& those alive
still
i didn't find you
i asked the clerk
if he had kept you tied down
or does he use your books
as dartboards
he smirked then shouted

(sky enters, wearing a white mask & imitates the clerk)

SKY: she's in the black section
to the back

BLAISE: even literature has its ghettos
stacked
along langston nikki & countee
maya who looked mad
the blues had her bad
zake tell me
did you demand to be segregated
does color modify poetry
i asked the manager
he patted me
whispered

SKY: *(imitates the manager)*
it's always been this way

BLAISE: ntozake shange

SKY: it's always been this way

BLAISE: ntozake shange

SKY: it's always been this way

BLAISE: ntozake shange

(blaise becomes hysterical, frightened by sky & he exits/ a picture of the first page of the constitution of the united states is projected on the screen as sky removes the white mask & chants)

SKY: IT'S ALWAYS BEEN THIS WAY
IN AMERICA
A PARODY OF THE GREATEST COUNTRY
IT NEVER WAS
BUT COULD STILL BE
IF WE DIDN'T KEEP STEALING
FROM THE BASIC FIBER
FRIGHTENED TO FACE A WHOLE CANVAS
WHERE ALL COLORS BLEND

(rock enters/as he speaks to sky, nile enters in an unrecognizable swirl of black crinoline & horse mask; awe-inspiring & somewhat diabolic, he portrays the horse in rock's next sketch, at times sinking to the ground, quiet, & at other times, he bounces back, revivified)

ROCK: often
trying to rid myself of
this black gay image
i galloped after the alternative
like a harnessed horse collapsed

in draft apologies foamed
at the mouth bitter

one morning
in the catskills i looked at
the sun
the birds
the trees
the river
myself

ever since
i ride on life
just as i am
hungry for ground
i eat this black gay nitty gritty
whole in its elements
something just meant to be

(nile exits in a swirl of black magic rock exits with sky as blaise
enters/ standing next to a phallic statue, blaise reminisces)

BLAISE: i want to celebrate vicious officious cocks
that kind with a hook or mushroom head
cast spells
made me lose consciousness when most alive
forced to acquiesce
grace under pressure
holiness in being truly low

i want to celebrate cushiony groins
hot balls a mouthful
tough titties with clip marks
hairy fists armed with a magic twist

which knew no limits
& this well-greased ass here
that took pleasure in its added dimensions

i want to celebrate masterful fantasies worshipped whole
top-training tricks kicks & licks
all those last calls
a stranger's smile posed no danger
then in my instinct i trusted
a past i ransack
now my conscience & my hands are my best friends

*(blaise exits as rock enters with a bottle of red wine/ he opens
the bottle, pours wine into a chalice & as he drinks, he recalls a
memory)*

ROCK: we wanted wine
the simple charm of a bottle
the toasts
the bouquet
a melody for memory
our fears never faded with a kiss
there's madness this moment

(the bottle accidentally falls & breaks, spilling wine on the floor)

the bottle falls
in a ritual of threats
sharp shards cut
we are suckers for each other's
spilled blood

*(rock exits/ nile enters/ he dips his finger in the wine spills & he too
recalls a memory/ sky enters & catches nile's train of thought/ the*

next sketch is enacted between sky who narrates it, nile who por-
trays himself & rock who will play the masked attacker)

SKY: he is often startled out of deep sleep when someone steps on
the grate six stories below: a cat jumps out of a garbage can, kids
crash beer bottles, even when the window rattles in the wind, he is
so startled that he gasps for breath as if all air blew out of him/ in
a flash

(nile pulls out a nine-inch ceremonial knife from his pocket)

he pulls out the nine-inch knife under his pillow—the nine-inch knife
sharpened & soaked regularly in vinegar with red-hot chili peppers,
the nine-inch knife he hopes will come in handy—he sits on the bed,
straight, still/ he waits twenty minutes; an hour or two; many times
until daybreak when he kisses the knife softly, puts it back under his
pillow, rolls up his body like a ball, crawling unto himself, alone with
memories & the pain of that night, so long ago now/

NILE: like most new york city august nights, treacherous/ with no
air conditioner & no fan, the heat made me twist in bed/ i got up
about midnight, changed the sweat-drenched sheets, pulled up the
shades, opened wide the fire-escape window—the only window in
the bedroom—

SKY: even a breeze was a hard bargain to wish for

NILE: but at least, i could view the full moon

SKY: toast it with cheap white wine which can cool you up/ make
you feel good fast like nothing else does/ indeed, he lay naked on
fresh-smelling baby-blue satin sheets, the full moon beamed down
dreams upon him/

(rock comes on stage, dressed as the masked attacker e.g. ski mask & gloves)

suddenly, he felt fingers lock around his neck/ he panicked/ tried to scream but the fingers were choking him/ he kicked mad, pushed the attacker aside, knelt on the bed, looking for anything to whack the attacker's head with when he heard him growl:

ROCK: if you make one more move, i'll can your fuckin face, you little faggot/

SKY: the attacker hammered his foot into nile's spine, pinning him down on the bed while he twisted his arms behind his back/

ROCK: yeah, i been watchin' you wiggle your faggot's ass

SKY: he said

ROCK: walkin with them airs, baby, i been wantin that piece sometime

SKY: nile couldn't move so he slightly turned his head to look at the attacker; if he might recognize him from somewhere/ all he saw was that big body/ moist glistening eyes peered out of a dark ski mask/ he smelled whiskey/ that look frightened him most/ nile trembled/

ROCK: i told you don't move

SKY: the attacker yelled, backhanded him across the head/ smack/ his jaw cracked/ he coughed out three teeth one after the other & kept moaning:

NILE: take anything you want just don't hurt me/ please don't hurt me/ please/

SKY: the attacker kept yelling

ROCK: bitch, i told you be quiet/ shut up/

SKY: smack/

ROCK: shut your stupid mouth, you little faggot/ shut up/(Beat)/ now you're really gettin my juice flowin/ i'm gonna stick it to you good/

SKY: the attacker bit him hard on the ass/ nile screamed/ the attacker grabbed the pillow, put it all over his head, spread-eagled him, lunged & plunged/

(rock exits down the aisle)

NILE: muffled cries . . .
stifled sighs . . .

(nile tries to stand up)

hours later, when he woke up, blood seeping out of his swollen eyes, blood seeping out of his broken nose, blood seeping out of his twisted lips, he tried to stand up but his knees buckled/ he couldn't walk/ he couldn't talk/ he dragged himself slowly across the floor to the window, climbed on the sill & passed out again/ at bellevue, someone told him some school girl had seen his naked body hanging on the fire-escape, a wine bottle sticking out of his ass & called the cops/
     ever since, every night, he checks the double locks/ he checks that the window is shut tight/ he checks that the nine-inch knife is where it must be & he slips into this state of siege/

(by now, nile has totally slipped into a nightmare/ brandishing the knife, he runs downstage & screams)

307

NILE: strike up music
music that'll take me out
of the middle of this tunnel
where i've been looking for the moon
since high noon
strike up music
music to get me higher
on a starship comet
6 flying saucers blaze at my trail
18,000,000 eyes 3-D
my move out of the big apple
into the world
ain't no magic below
america
what kind of bad card
did we draw
strike up music
music & please hold the tears
bernard goetz
i got no time
to hear bullets ricochet
i'm way past pelham bay parkway
so i don't have to make sense
out of everybody's philosophy
scrawled boldly in front of me
whatever it is
i give you all my very best wishes
got to go about my business
see
feel
nothing earthy
neptune

are you listening
can we talk
information

*(shaking & sobbing, sky takes nile in his arms/ nile breaks away/
the stage goes to darkness expect for a special on nile who's slowly
advancing downstage, brandishing the knife, almost menacing the
audience/ sky walks over to nile & gently takes the knife away from
him/ lights come up/ nile walks away & sits in a corner/ the jingle of
the carousel plays as sky speaks)*

SKY: sometimes
the sky opens up
my spirit jumps high
& my heart pumps with happiness
like when i clap my hands in the church choir
lead the congregation along in harmony
sing lyrics god sends me
the whole world shakes in my tambourine
or when i warm the disco floor
sweat oozes
no polemics
no antics
no politics
just immediacy of the music
this ecstasy got grit
once a year
i take amtrak
back to the red clay hills of georgia
my sister greets me with great big hugs
& a hot meal
nobody bakes chops like miss belzora carter
106 penelope avenue
augusta

come with me
you'll dog them thick oniony things down
i do mean down
lick your plate spit-clean
feel no shame
or like real-close closeness
the kind that gets my heart to skip beats
when i kiss
the magic of candle light
makes me & my beau glow
the room swoon as johnny mathis croons
but nothing brings
this fresh-flower freak here
more natural-high than springtime

(sky sits on stage/ with the knife he turns the soil around the pine tree)

i be crawling
digging in the dirt
seeding
cutting
rerooting
planting
watering
for the entire summer
my garden smells
from here to heaven
when i rest my ears to the ground
there's peace in this place
i soak up all these moments
treasure them forever

*(the jingle of the carousel fades out as firecrackers explode/ nile
becomes very agitated)*

NILE: whenever thunder rolls
the whole world closes in
on me
mirrors shatter
i hear grandma whisper
like she used to when i was a kid
in new orleans

SKY: (*imitates nile's grandmother, then hums as nile speaks*) oya
gonna strike free

NILE: then she chants
till thunder is rain water
music which stretches my mind
to no limits
& meets deep seas
cast off that loose with yemanja
ready to tell all
i'm the impossible black homosexual
drowning in the american dream
s.o.s. for you & i
to swim against the stream
wash up our lives
in tradition we lost
cosmic magic
till thunder is rain water
music

(*nile picks up a sacred pitcher & sprinkles water on the wine/ blood
    spills & around the pine tree, calling back a spirit from the dead/
    he sprinkles water on sky who unearths a small urn under the pine
    tree/ nile exits/ sky opens the urn, opens it & takes out a small plas-
    tic bag/ as he unties the bag, he says:*)

SKY: there were no tears/ there was no time for tears that year/ just a tight knot in the pit of my chest where it hurts more each day/ yet, it had all come to this: a two-pound plastic bag filled with ash, bits of bones, fragments of teeth that didn't completely burn/ it had all come too quick/

it seems only yesterday, riis park bustled with laughter & w.b.l.s. blasted music everywhere/ beautiful bodies languished on the sand in colorful swimwear/ volleyball players, joggers ran up & down/ lifeguards whistled swimmers who strayed too far/ vendors hawked pepsi & ice cream sandwiches, cheap cologne & fake gold bracelets/ that days of wine & smiles, we were all walking on sunshine/

next to me on the "i love new york" beach mat, dreads cascading down his head, duke eased through his one hundred daily push-ups/ every inch of his six-foot taut body glistened deliciously like honey/ many a passing glance sized him up but the dude was all mine & had been mine for ten years/ he was so fine that i paid no attention to a spot on his left foot, right below his big toe–a spot, small, purple like the stain of a crushed grape/

soon after, it multiplied like stars in early evening/ like buds on a tree in early spring, it multiplied all over his feet, his legs, up his ass, inside his intestines, all over his face, his neck, down his throat, inside his brains/ for nine months of fever & wracking coughs, nine months of sweat & shaking chills, nine months of diarrhea & jerking spasms, they multiplied, wrenched him skinny like a spider, a body of pain/

(blaise enters quietly, wearing a death mask [white-painted face, half-slit eyes under heavy lids, crooked mouth]; he will play the part of duke)

BLAISE: sky, i don't understand this/ i don't want to understand this/

SKY: popped out of duke as he came out of the anesthesia/

BLAISE: i'm sick of this hose in n y nose/ i'm sick of this tube in my
dick/ all these IVs in my arms/ i'n sick of being strapped to this bed/

SKY: he coughed out a scream/ ea sy, easy baby i whispered, smoothing my gloved hand over his head the side they hadn't shaved for
the biopsy, glad he was starting t ouble again/ i bet he could see my
smile behind the mask they made me wear/

BLAISE: i ain't joking/ i am tired/

SKY: he said

BLAISE: & i'd rather be dead/

SKY: sir duke, don't you talk like hat/ you ain't gonna die/ you're
only thirty-one/ you're too young o die/ we gonna beat this shit,
i kept repeating/ that's why i wan you to come home where you
belong/ two month's too freaking ong to stay cooped up in this
room/ this hospital food ain't fit f r a dog/ i'm gonna make you
strong/ we gonna cheat death, yoι hear me/ sky & duke, hooked for
life/ come on say it like we used tι sing all the time/

BLAISE: Sky

SKY: he muttered

BLAISE: i'm gonna die/

SKY: no no no, i kept yelling in th corridor, running to the nurse's
station where three of them stood

ROCK (as head nurse)
mr carter, calm down/ i told you r ιany times before that you should
dispose of your gloves & your gow n as soon as you leave the room/

313

SKY: the head nurse said as she rushed into duke's room with another nurse/ what's the number for the administrator on duty? i asked this tiny filipino nurse/ i want to take my lover home/

NILE (enters quietly & plays the part of the filipino nurse)
take him home, what do you mean?

SKY: she asked/ i believe i'm speaking english/ i said i want to take him home/

NILE: but your friend is dying/ the biopsy showed kaposi's/

SKY: you are killing him/ you & all this hospital ain't doing shit for him/ idiots! you should be ashamed of yourselves/

ROCK: mr. carter

SKY: the head nurse said as she walked back/

ROCK: stop it/ stop this nonsense right now & i mean it

SKY: the head nurse said as she walked back.

ROCK: you ain't gonna come here in my ward & upset my staff/ is that understood?

SKY: i kept quiet & looked past her as the filipino nurse walked away/

ROCK: mr. carter, I'm still waiting for an answer/

SKY: yes, understood/

ROCK: you can do all the screaming you want, loud as you need but from now on, you do it outside. That's where you should be carrying

314

on in the first place/ it's obvious to a duck that if enough of you homosexuals were acting up in the streets, those politicians & all the others would be taking you quite seriously & allocate much more money for research/ i don't have to teach you history/ you told me you was born in the south, & brother, if most of us in the 50s and 60s didn't get into civil disobedience, march-ins, sit-ins & what have you, we would still be riding in the back of the bus/

SKY: you should really talk, sister/ really/ you're probably one of those black folks who think that we gays are getting just what we deserve/

ROCK: now that's way beneath you & i won't bother to dignify that with an answer/ better yet, look . . . look around/ you see all these little cabinets outside these rooms/ i don't have to tell you what's in these little cabinets or why they're standing outside these rooms, do i/ count them/ go ahead, count them/ that's right, nine/ nine rooms with AIDS patients in a ward of seventeen beds/ nine/ eight young men & one young lady who's so demented, the poor thing don't even know her own name/ you think i like to see all this misery/ you think it don't break my heart to be messed up in all this hopelessness/ i don't like this/ i'm telling you i don't like it one bit but all of us in this hospital are trying to do the very best we can under these circumstances/ unfortunately that ain't enough but lord help us all/ why, why don't you go get some rest/ you'll be doing your friend & yourself a disservice if you continue this vigil/ come, come on sit down & drink some water/

SKY: she filled a paper cup & put it to my lips/

ROCK: it's alright

SKY: she said

ROCK: honey, i understand/

SKY: & she held me/

from then on, i wasted no time/ duke's too weak now but in a week
he could be home/ he did consent after much convincing, insisting
that i take down all twelve mirrors hanging on every single wall in
the apartment/ my indefinite leave of absence was approved rather
quickly/ ever since i had told my co-workers about duke's illness
& why i had been so stressed, they've been wiping the unit's phone
with alcohol/ this year, they even asked me to bring liquor to the
christmas party instead of my tasty fritters they used to love/ at
times, saved some for their kids/ i took a bank loan/ said it was
for continuing education/ i rented a wheel chair, a walker and a
commode/ i bought sheepskin pillows, a portable suction machine,
a stand-up bed tray, hot water bottles, all kinds of medical supplies and bundles of paper towels/ with coupons and duke's food
stamps, i stacked up the refrigerator/ i vacuumed, dusted and
waxed the parquet floor/ i called on friends and neighbors to volunteer for chores/ my sister belzora, a retired nurse said that she'd
come up from georgia/ instead of a hard narrow bed in a sterile
room, duke would die in the dignity and the beauty of his own
home, on our big brass bed/

    sir duke, do you remember the first time we met at peter rabbit? i
asked him the night he came home as we sat on the living-room sofa,
like we liked to, his head resting on my chest/

BLAISE: how could i forget/ you & your bunch of loud friends were
bitching at the bar, singing all them old ballads so off-key/ sky, you
were stoned-drunk/

SKY: i was not/ i was just enjoying a nice sunday evening & besides,
you're the one who walked in there with them tight bell-bottom
jeans & yellow platform shoes, got everybody's heart just pumping
& jumping/ child, you looked so good & when the d.j. played "hooked
for life," i had to ask you to dance/

316

that night we played "hooked for life" over & over, sang, even danced a bit/ two disco divas with ten years of memories: the trips, the parties, the steps, the orgies . . . laughter/

BLAISE: Sky

SKY: he muttered as i tucked him in bed & kissed him good night

BLAISE: i'm glad i'm home/

SKY & BLAISE: i love you/ thanks for all the good times/

BLAISE: i love you/

SKY: time was running out/ days went by/ duke made a will & named me executor of his estate/ he couldn't get up or eat by himself/ belzora flew in as she had promised/ she fixed all those deep-southern meals duke used to like but could hardly eat/ he'd stare at the wall with a glazed far-away look, eyes sunken way back/
    nights went by/ he gagged, choked & vomited/ i helped him sit up & cough, massaged his back, washed him up, changed his diapers, smoothed the bed sheets, caressed him until he fell asleep then woke up again from a nightmare, struggling for air/ every four hours, belzora would give him shots of morphine to soothe the pain/
    the doctor came in one day & said that he didn't expect duke to live through the week/ his mother doris whom i had called despite duke forbidding me to, flew from chicago/ she came huffing & puffing, waving her finger in my face/

ROCK: what you done to my baby? what you done now to duke? where is he? i want to see . . .

SKY: i ain't taking you into the bedroom until you calm down. duke's too sick & much too weak to put up with your jive/

ROCK: who do you think you are, talking to me like that? i'm his mother & i have a right to . . .

SKY: you ain't moving from this living-room/ woman, you & i got some serious business to talk about/

ROCK: you ain't got nothing to say to me i want to hear/ you have perverted my son, low down immoral . . .

SKY: don't you ever, ever talk to me about morality/ not ever/ you have been blessed with four sons but as i understand, each one by a different father & you ain't ever been married/

ROCK: shut your dirty mouth before you say things even god can't forgive you for

SKY: she yelled, lifting her hands as if to strike me/ don't you try it, i said, holding back her arms & putting my hands over her mouth to muffle her screams/ go ahead, why don't you go on & bite me/ i mean you'll get blood in your mouth & who knows, i might be infected too/ go ahead/ you'll see if this disease discriminates between gays & straights/ don't you want to find out/ go right ahead/ take a big bite/ i kept taunting her/ she froze/

    now, you're finally going to hear me out/ yes, you will, i told her, restraining her as she tried to move away/

    i met you once, nine years ago thanksgiving, when duke & i went to chicago, on our very first trip together/ you didn't like me then & you still don't like me/ i didn't like you then & i still don't like you/ damn it, i was willing to give you a chance because you are duke's mother & i respected that/ you were so mean when he told you about our relationship/ you ordered him to break up with me & move back to chicago because new york city was corrupting him/ i bet you didn't think i knew about that one/ he was all sobs & tears on our flight back/ i remember that sunday night, he couldn't wait to get to the dorm, to call you/ you should have seen him shaking from all those mean things you were saying to him on the phone/ how you didn't want anything more to do with him if he didn't repent/ how you couldn't have such a sinner as a son/ he was so broken & it hurt me that you had hurt him so/ i couldn't believe that a mother would actually be that cruel/ woman, he loved you but he loved me too/ i remember i took him in my arms, rocked him all night long/ right then & there, we promised each other that we were going to be together forever; hooked for life/ so we both helped each other through graduation/ i got involved with a record company & he became a damn good accountant/ we rented this apartment & been living together ever since, man & man/ doris, i have been good to your son & duke has been so good to me, in ways you can't even begin to imagine/ i don't expect you to like it but this is our story, just the way it is . . .

it was then & only then, that i released her from my grip/

ROCK: can i see my baby now?

SKY: she whispered

that friday at 3:00 p.m. while his mother sat on the bed—holding his left hand & read the twenty-third psalm—i sat on the bed, holding his right hand & relived all our good memories—trusting the instant, duke yielded his soul/

(sky tries to fight the tears but can't stop himself)

there were no tears/ there was no time for tears that year/ just a tight knot in the pit of my chest where it hurts more each day/ yet, it had all come to this: a two-pound plastic bag filled with a promise gone, scattered dreams, can't even pick up the pieces, all too quick/

*(sky is overcome with emotions & runs downstage/ grace jones'
version of "la vie en rose" plays/nile dances with rock/ after the
long instrumental at the beginning of the song, blaise removes
the death mask & robe/ in full grace jones drag, he lip-synchs
the song & mimics grace jones to perfection as he moves around
nile & rock/ in the middle instrumental, in a very deep amplified
voice, blaise speaks)*

BLAISE: once in a dream
america was 200,000,000 hearts
each shining like a satellite
each shining bright in each other's light
each shining in its own right
i was sun
now i have a nightmare
& it's a nightmare deeply rooted in the american dream
my normal heart just ain't ticking as is
i'm a time bomb

*(projections of martin luther king & harvey milk's pictures along with
a slide of the perfect rows of graves at arlington cemetery are shown/
one by one, nile & rock drop dead onstage, emitting loud cries/ sky
observes all this & observes himself caught in this madness/ blaise
grabs the american flag from the pine tree & waves it over the dead
bodies, turning & taunting them as he keeps shouting)*

i'm a time bomb
i'm a time bomb
i'm a time bomb

*(the song winds down/ blaise kisses the rose & puts it next to the
pine tree & the bag of ash/ blaise too falls dead, waving the flag/ sky
walks over to the dead bodies, picks up the flag & chants)*

SKY: DARKNESS
INFINITY
INERTNESS
NOTHING

(lights dim except for a special on sky who sings the song LIGHT)

SKY: HOURS OF DARKNESS
HOURS OF HELPLESSNESS
LOST IN SHADOWS
WHERE IS THE LIGHT

HOURS OF COLDNESS
HOURS OF EMPTINESS
STRIPPED & FRIGHTENED
WHERE IS THE LIGHT

LIGHT, LET THERE BE LIGHT
LIGHT, GIVE US MORE LIGHT
IN OUR HEARTS, IN OUR SOULS
LET THERE BE LIGHT

HOURS OF SADNESS
HOURS OF LONELINESS
HURT & BROKEN
WHERE IS THE LIGHT

HOURS OF MADNESS
HOURS OF BITTERNESS
CAUGHT AT CROSSROADS
WHERE IS THE LIGHT

LIGHT, LET THERE BE LIGHT
LIGHT, GIVE US MORE LIGHT

IN OUR HEARTS, IN OUR SOULS
LET THERE BE LIGHT

IN OUR HEARTS, IN OUR SOULS
LET THERE BE LIGHT
IN OUR HEARTS
IN OUR SOULS
LET THERE BE LIGHT

*(sky rings a double-iron bell to call the gods/ a ball of light flashes in the
pine tree/ it's the light of duke's spirit merging with that of the statue
of liberty & the pine tree/ blinded, sky unleashes a primal scream
which shakes & wakes up the company from the nightmare/ the ball of
light quickly disappears/ rock is the first to stand up & speak)*

ROCK: ever since this health crisis started, i have engaged myself
more & more in the reality of our lives yet dwelt in so many ques-
tions/ where do we fit in the reactionary new age of america? where
do we fit in a racist gay society? in a homophobic black one? what do
we believe in? what makes us live?

lacking any real sense of black gay history, probing every tidbit
of early memories, gossip, secrets, stories/ looking for truth & a folk-
lore all our own, i've been at my wits' end, grasping empty air/

all winter long, i hiked across america to feel for myself the
mood of the country/ returning to new york city, full of disap-
pointment, anger & disbelief at how far we had come as a nation
yet how backward we're moving, i stopped in baltimore, the city
where i was born/ the city i had left in tears, still in my teens,
right after ma's funeral & that major argument with pa about
all these fairies i ran around with, vowing never to return, not
even when he died six years ago/ there, i visited uncle roy, pa's
younger brother who had moved in with us when he came back
from world war 2, blind & disabled/

just as i remembered him, a short slightly built jolly man, always

in bright-color clothes & shiny army boots, a silk scarf tied around
his neck, no teeth now yet a smile a mile wide, with his dark glasses,
wooden cane, smelling forever of old spice, uncle roy used to gather
all my cousins, my sisters & me/ we kids would listen with such
eager ears to his tales/ when ma would say: "roy robinson, when
you gonna grow up? you is no teenager"/ he'd shout back in rasping
laughter: "why should i? kids don't jump rope like i do"/ you should
have seen him hop on one leg, two, doing the double-dutch/ it was
so funny/ early on, i suspected uncle roy was in the life/ one thing i
knew for sure, he is enjoying life/

never a complaint, never a raised voice, uncle roy read palms &
could tell the future or what kind of person you were just by a hand-
shake/ a firm one meant you were ambitious/ a weak one, wishy-
washy/ a high-five, you were up to no good/ so when he predicted
that i'd be a sculptor, took me to the art supply store that day &
bought me a red box full of tools, i was too thrilled/ he said to me as
he took my little hands in his: "go ahead, rock, sculpt what's real to
you"/ & i did just that/

pa had a fit & ma fainted when they came home & found out that
i too had gone to work/ on the living-room furniture that is/ i had
sculpted rainbows & cows, stars & pigs, martians with big eyes &
chickens hatching big eggs, flying angels & little boys, black boys
everywhere/

we laughed so hard at the serious whipping pa had adminis-
tered to my ass that night which was not funny then cause those
cheeks burned for six days straight & pa forbade uncle roy to
play with us kids on account that he was a bad influence on our
impressionable minds/

we swapped stories that night/ i shared with him my ups &
downs/ in the morning, he took me to the cemetery/ he pointed out
the plot where he wanted to be buried between grandma's pink
grave & ma's which was next to pa's/ right before i left for the train
station, he said: "son, whenever you're down deep in darkness & you
feel you can't go on, let that little light in your soul shine/ let it shine

& it will take you home"/ then he put his hands all over my face, over my head, my shoulders, my chest/ touching him was fantastic but being touched by him was magic/

(rock picks a handful of dirt from the ground & mixes it with the ash in the plastic bag)

i want to break new ground & mold myself a brand new community of black gays standing up once & for all in realization, validation & celebration of ourselves/ a brand-new community of black gays aspiring to the visions we have for ourselves/ a brand-new community of black gays singing a new love song not just for america but for ourselves/

i see the possibility of my creation begins with us, touching ourselves/ in touch, there's feeling

NILE: healing

SKY: togetherness

ROCK: a safe promise
BLAISE: the light we've been looking for

ROCK: & can follow home, home to this garden in our soul where once again, we root ourselves/

(rock anoints himself with the mixture of dirt & ash then anoints the others/sky walks over to the pine tree & cuts some branches which he gives to each member of the company/ they form a close, tight circle as they become brothers through a rite of earth-sharing, stomping the floor, dancing with the branches, clapping their hands/ sky starts to speak as the others continue to dance, touch & heal each other/ the jingle of the carousel plays)

SKY: i have journeyed to macchu picchu
stood beneath the towering arches of the colosseum
called on amun-ra at karnak
climbed atop the many pyramids of mexico
crisscrossed africa
sat down from dawn to dusk on a stone in the acropolis
walked along the great wall of china
i have roamed the four corners of earth
ferreting out humanity's poetic essence
man dies
values endure
luckily alive
i sing out the soul of black gays in america
more than ever
i give aural dimensions to our visions
where black & gay is
an everyday necessity
transcending nothingness

(as the jingle of the carousel keeps playing, the company forms a procession through the aisles so they can spread their magic about & dominate what is to come/ blaise is first, carrying a candle/ next in line, nile bears the chalice of wine & the ceremonial knife/ then comes rock with the urn of ashes, followed by sky holding the flag/ after they've walked around the audience, they proceed back to the stage/ the jingle of the carousel & the lights fade out/ kneeling right where they had started, they chant)

SKY, NILE, ROCK & BLAISE: I AM THE ROOT
I OPEN THE EARTH
& PASS THROUGH IT
A HERO OF MY OWN MAKING
A HERO TO MYSELF
A HERO TO AMERICA

(sky stands up & closes the curtains/ he walks downstage
by himself)

SKY: my whole life has been a work in progress
searching for my elements
i wanted to share with you
this new love song

(sky sings the song "New Love Song" as a silent film of fireworks,
with the statue of liberty gleaming in light, rolls)

SKY: MISSING THE DREAMS, THEY WERE BURNT OUT TOO FAST
MISSING THE JOY THAT WAS NOT MEANT TO LAST
WALKING IN SMOKE ON THE ASH OF OUR PAST
I WANT TO SING A NEW LOVE SONG

NEW LOVE SONG, FLOWING LIKE A JET STREAM
NEW LOVE SONG, WASHING ALL OVER ME
I WANT TO SING A NEW LOVE SONG
I WANT TO SING A NEW LOVE SONG
STRIPPING MY HEART OF THESE LAYERS OF PAIN
STRIPPING MY HEART OF THESE MEMORIES THAT DRAIN
STANDING ALONE & EXPOSED ONCE AGAIN
I WANT TO SING A NEW LOVE SONG

NEW LOVE SONG, FLOWING LIKE A JET STREAM
NEW LOVE SONG, WASHING ALL OVER ME
I WANT TO SING A NEW LOVE SONG
I WANT TO SING A NEW LOVE SONG

TIMELINE

1957

*Born on October 2 in Cap-Haïtien, Haiti, named Yves François Lubin. His mother was Marie Myriam Lubin, a registered nurse anesthetist. Saint's father, Dr. Mercier, had asked Marie to abort Yves after the unwed couple discovered they were expecting. Yves did not meet his father until he was an adult. Yves lived with his mother and maternal grandparents in Les Cayes, Haiti.

1965

*Grandmother passes away and mother moves to Geneva, Switzerland.

*Remains in Haiti and moves in with his aunt, Marcelle Lubin-Hall.

1970

*Visits his mother in a life-changing trip to New York, where she has relocated, and settles in Queens Village.

1974

*After graduating from Jamaica High School in Queens, Yves enrolls as a pre-med student at Queens College, but drops out soon after.

*Becomes a dancer with the Martha Graham Dance Company.

1978

*Starts work at the New York City Health and Hospitals Corporation.

1980

*Stops performing with the Martha Graham Dance Company after sustaining an injury.

*Chooses the name Assotto Saint. Assotto is the Creole pronunciation of a drum in used in vodou ritual (at one point, took to spelling Assotto with one "t" but superstitiously added back the other "t" when his CD4 t-cell count dropped to nine). Saint is derived from Toussaint L'Ouverture, one of his heroes.

*Becomes a member of the Blackheart Collective, a group of Black gay writers and visual artists created to give voice to Black gay expression and provide a unique perspective on the issues of the day. They produced several printed journals of art, poetry and prose including *Yemonja* and *Prison Issue*.

Risin' to the Love We Need wins second prize from the Jane Chambers Award for Gay and Lesbian Playwriting.

*In November, falls in love with Jan Urban Holmgren, a Swedish-born composer with whom he began collaborating on a number of theatrical and musical projects. Their relationship would last thirteen years.

*Cofounds the Metamorphosis Theater with Holmgren.

1981

*Moves to Chelsea in Manhattan.

*Collaborates with Holmgren as a techno pop band called Xotika.

Risin' to the Love We Need premieres on September 11, presented by the Stonewall Repertory Theater at Courtyard Playhouse.

1983
*Performs his solo performance piece *Coupon Queen.*

1984
*Performs his solo performance piece *Black Fag* on August 22 at 8BC, a performance space in the Lower East Side.

1985
*Stars in the film *Loisaida Lusts* by Ela Troyano and Uzi Parnes, filmed on the Lower East Side. Plays the role of Jean, a dancer.

1986
*Becomes a US citizen.

*Pens an autobiographical piece called *The Impossible Black Homosexual (OR Fifty Ways To Become One)*, wherein he writes that "on the day he naturalized as an American citizen [he] sat naked on the current president's picture and after he was finished called the performance 'Bushshit'"

*Becomes a founding member of Other Countries, a not-for-profit organization formed by a collective of Black gay male writers in New York City with the purpose to develop, promote, communicate, and cultivate literary, cultural, and social endeavors and pursuits relevant to the experience of Black gay men.

*Work appears in *In The Life: A Black Gay Anthology*, edited by Joseph Beam (Alyson Books).

1987
*Becomes a member of ACT UP.

*Publishes his chapbook *Triple Trouble* in *Tongues Untied* (GMP, London).

*Work is published in *New Men, New Minds*, edited by Franklin Abbott (The Crossing Press).

*On October 10th, joins a mass wedding on the National Mall in Washington, DC, with Holmgren. Designed to reflect an alternative approach to love and marriage, "The Wedding," part of the March on Washington for Gay and Lesbian Rights, rejected the narrow definition of heterosexual marriage.

*In November, Saint and Holmgren are diagnosed with HIV.

1988
*Serves as poetry editor for the anthology *Other Countries: Black Gay Voices*, published by Other Countries Collective.

*Publishes poetry in *Gay and Lesbian Poetry in Our Time*, edited by Carl Morse and Joan Larkin (St. Martins Press).

1989
*Premieres *New Love Song* in February at the 18th Street Playhouse in Chelsea.

*Establishes his own publishing company, Galiens Press (a compression of the words *gay* and *aliens*), and uses it as a platform to publish work exclusively by gay Black poets.

*Galiens Press publishes *Stations*, Saint's first collection of poetry.

1990
*Receives the Fellowship in Poetry from the New York Foundation of the Arts and the James Baldwin Award from the Black Gay Leadership Forum.

*Xotica's wacky and transgressive dance track called "Forever Gay" is released on a compilation CD, *Feeding The Flame: Songs By Men To End AIDS* (Flying Fish Records).

*Stages and performs *Nuclear Lovers* theater piece

*Holmgren is diagnosed with AIDS.

1991
*Galiens Press publishes *The Road Before Us: 100 Gay Black Poets*.

*Work appears in *Brother to Brother: New Writings by Black Gay Men*, edited by Essex Hemphill (Alyson Publications). Conceived by Joseph Beam.

*Is diagnosed with AIDS.

*Stops working at New York City Health and Hospitals Corporation.

1992
The Road Before Us: 100 Gay Black Poets wins the Lambda Literary Award for Gay Poetry.

*At fellow Black gay poet Donald W. Woods' funeral, openly confronts Woods' family for their hypocritical elision of Woods's gayness; is especially outraged since Woods had fought to end the repressive forms of silence that equal death for gay individuals and people with AIDS. Stands up and "testifies" on his brother's behalf.

*Galiens Press publishes *Here To Dare: 10 Gay Black Poets*.

*Holmgren retires from American Airlines after twenty-five years.

1993

*Holmgren dies of complications due to AIDS.

*In October, attends the March on Washington to deliver a quilt dedicated to Holmgren, which was included as part of the NAMES Project AIDS Memorial Quilt. While delivering to the quilt panel, encloses a copy of Jan's funeral program along with a note: "I made this quilt for my 13-year life-partner, Jan Urban Holmgren. He was my Jan & my man. Born in Alno, Sweden, on April 25, 1939, he died in my arms on March 29, 1993. We both found out in late 1987 that we were HIV-positive. Jan came down with full-blown AIDS in early 1990. I came down with full-blown AIDS in late 1991. Yes, it is a strange phenomenon when both life-partners in a relationship are fatally ill. Because of my disbelief in God & a spiritual after-life, it gives me great pleasure to know that at least we will be physically reunited in the same grave at The Evergreens Cemetery in Brooklyn, NY."

*Joins other AIDS activists in the Ashes Action on October 11 while still in DC, where protesters sprinkled the cremated remains of people with AIDS inside the White House gate. Is arrested, spends the night in jail, and appears before the judge the following day, Monday, October 12.

*Is published in *Sojourner: Black Gay Voices in the Age of AIDS* (Other Countries Press).

*Appears in Emmy and Peabody Award–winning filmmaker Marlon Riggs's film, *Non, Je Ne Regrette Rien (No Regret)*, in which five Black gay men with AIDS talk about how they came to terms with the disease.

1994

*Dies of AIDS-related complications on June 29 at the age of thirty-six.

*A memorial is held on the Fourth of July at Redden's Funeral Home. The funeral service is held the next day at the Metropolitan-Duane United Methodist Church. Is buried with Jan at the Evergreens Cemetery in Brooklyn, New York.

*Galiens Press publishes *Wishing for Wings* posthumously.

*Is published in *Jugular Defences: An AIDS Anthology edited by Peter Daniels and Steve Anthony* (Oscars Press, London)

1995

*Though Saint himself has passed, his contributions continue to live on; he is nominated for a Lambda Literary Award for *Wishing For Wings*.

Milking Black Bull: 11 Gay Black Poets, a collection conceived by Saint, is published by Vega Press.

*His work appears in *The Name of Love: Classic Gay Love Poems*, edited by Michael Lassell (St. Martin's Press).

1996

Spells of a Voodoo Doll: The Poems, Fiction, Essays and Plays of Assotto Saint is published as A Richard Kasak Book and subsequently nominated for a Lambda Literary Award in the Gay Biography or Autobiography category.

2008

*His mother dies on November 11.

TRIBUTES

I met Yves in early 1986 through our mutual friend Michael Evans. Our bond deepened as we cared for Michael whose battle with AIDS began later that year—Michael would die in March of '89. Yves and I chatted quietly as we took turns sitting with Michael while he received his IV drips. We spoke about activism, life, and literature, as we stood in the long, lonely hallways of the hospital or waited into the night in visitor's lounges. I came to know Yves as an empathetic, brave, and caring person; a devoted and tireless friend to many and my closest friend. We exchanged ideas about our writing, and he helped me with my first book, *A Journal of the Plague Years: Poems 1979-1992*, as I helped him with his last book of poems, *Wishing for Wings*.

I admired Yves' calm, knowledgeable manner with the physicians and nurses who were often hurriedly inexact, overly conciliatory, and occasionally patronizing to this slightly effeminate Haitian-American man. But Yves always demanded to be listened to and inspired respect. He wore a neatly trimmed mustache and spoke with a distinct French creole accent that carried a pronounced inflection and lilt. Measured in speech, he parsed his words thoughtfully and slowly with a fluid musicality. His face glowed with a thin smile of agreement when some answer or comment pleased him or reflected perplexity at some particular friend's foolish actions, which to Yves seemed politically or socially ill-advised. Because Yves tended to be quiet in private conversation. I was always amazed at his flamboyance, his fiery, fierce, and eloquent voice in activist meetings and performances.

At home, Yves would lean his head back, close his eyes softly deliberating as he gazed upward before suddenly shaking his head, clicking his tongue, and calling out myriad injustices, hypocrisies, bullshit of all kinds with precision and wit. I remember him seated at his Brother electric typewriter, working through the night to get out the galleys for Galiens Press, finish the play scripts for Metamorphosis Theater, and write heartfelt speeches as he battled homophobia, intolerance, and racism, fighting for our survival in a time of horrible plague.

Walter Holland

*

The road before us looms as an infernal horizon, then metamorphoses and appears as the cyclical Phoenix at the crossroads of life, an intersection of evolution and revolution, where we—baptized in the righteous anger of the Haitian Saint Assotto—forgive and heal in the knowledge that none of us is a cosmic orphan.
Je ne regrette rien!

André De Shields

*

I'm not sure where or how I met Assotto Saint, but I do know it was in the late eighties and most likely in connection with the anthology *Other Countries: Black Gay Voices* (at the Schomburg?). I was a fan of Assotto's work and inspired by his poetry and daring and bold performances downtown. We'd see one another at various BlackQueer events and would always celebrate one another. He was older than me by five years. I loved the drama of the leather lifestyle he brought with him and the bold accented diasporic perspective. He had deep connections with queer African and French speaking Caribbean and Dutch communities, and I had recently come back from living in Holland and France, so we bonded over that aspect of diaspora. At the time, many Black queer men who were partnered with Euro lovers eschewed Afrocentric spaces for more white gay spaces but Assotto fully brought all of themself everywhere!

Thomas Allen Harris

*

When I think of Assotto I think of a fierce, fabulous, frontrunner... I think he would read my shameless use of alliteration... I think he accomplished his mission of laying "one more stepping-stone on the road to gay black poetical empowerment"... he is missed, but his legacy lives on.

Djola Branner

*

The 1993 OutWrite's OutSpoken Series, curated by Michele, introduced me to the fabulous Assotto. The moment was filled with richness. Assotto's empowering words and mesmerizing performances captivated everyone. His mission was to bring forth not only his truths, but those from voices of the LGBTQ communities. I can envision Assotto saying, "Ou pa bezmen pe = Be not afraid!"

Philip Robinson

*

Assotto Saint, who we knew in the day-to-day as Yves Lubin, was daring, with a razor-sharp intellect, and a willingness to tell the truth about everything—family, love, sex, life as an immigrant from a poor but culturally rich country that he explored with love and devotion. His honesty scared me sometimes. Conforming to ideals of Black (gay) male masculinity seemed easier and safer. Yves was not easy and he was not safe. He challenged us as Black gay writers, and he rode with us until he could ride no longer.

Cary Alan Johnson

I will forever remember Assotto's courage to live his truth. From him, I learned at a young age to do the same. Assotto was a warm and kind spirit. The legacy of his work will endure and inspire many others.

Anthony Knight

*

With Yves, less was always more—the exact opposite approach he usually took with his sartorial style. I have a vivid recollection of Yves taking his pen to someone's draft and saying, "This can be cut. And this, and this, and this as well. There!"

Guy Mark Foster

*

Assotto Saint was a kaleidoscope of gaiety in all aspects of his individualities...

Stephen Booth

*

I met Assotto at the Other Countries writer's workshop. His commitment to the word and honesty was inspiring. "You are not seducing me with these fonts!" is a critique of his I've never forgotten—a simple message of "let the work speak for itself," as he did powerfully in his writing and too-short life.

G. Winston James

*

After the death of Jan, his partner, I watched Assotto
as we marched on NYC's Pride Day in the early '90s.
As bystanders cheered, his steely eyes stared down AIDS—the big bad
wolf who was devouring us. He was ready to rumble.

Steve Langley

*

Silence = Death. Writing = Life. Publishing = Survival.

His greatest ability as my editor, preceding publication of *The Road Before Us 100 Gay Black Poets* and beyond, was his gifted, world-view capacity for splicing the context of most any content to put the syntax into proper order.

He recognized the initial structure of my poem as an expression of vulnerability; while I considered the order of it to be more of a protest and act of poetic defiance.

I was livid with him until, importantly, he clarified that my intention was not at all lost; assuming no credit for arranging it to an eminently greater effect!

I remembered his compassion and stature today and I cried (and yes Yves, they were tears of JOY!!!). ~Snap!

Rickey Butler

*

Assotto and Jan hosted me whenever I was in NY. They were very gracious I must say. I met Yves (his name before Assotto) in '76. He somehow managed to get my phone number and called me to introduce himself to me; it was around the time I was just starting to blow up as a musician. They fixed me fabulous meals and took me to great restaurants. We went to bars and clubs most evenings. Every year I would learn new things about the city. We also went to many late-night shows. He introduced me to the catacombs. That same year he took me down Christopher Street to the piers to show me the devastation of AIDS. Almost ¾ of the businesses were closed; he said the business owners all died from AIDS. Jan had been dead for about a year and a half then.

Blackberri

*

Have long felt that I wouldn't or couldn't appreciate his work when read by someone other than him. No one else could match his presence, theatricality, sincerity, audacity, all mixed in Haitian accented rhythms. Without that, I suspect, those "vicious, officious cocks" he spoke of with such singular relish would only lay flat on the page. I miss him.

Allen Luther Wright

*

I remember being thrilled to be part of *The Road Before Us* as it was one of the first acceptances of my work. It still means a lot to me.

Reginald Harris

*

Determined that both his rage and his beauty speak—no shout out to anyone who heard him or read his work. There will be many that voice his words aloud, but no one will be as eloquent as he.

Bil (sic) Wright

*

His gifting me his manuscript *Risin'* for a reading I was to present in London, England.
His requesting one of my poems to publish.
His performing in the cult classic film *Loisaida Lusts.*
His telling me not to abandon *Other Countries* because they needed me.

Sur Rodney Sur

*

One of the great tragedies of the AIDS epidemic is the loss of Assotto Saint, so gifted as a writer and performer and such a strong presence. Not only did he create a significant body of work that is essential to the LGBTQ canon, but he encouraged others, especially queer men of color, to share their work. As fierce as he could be in his activism and performance, he was also a man who was a dear friend to those lucky to be close to him. He is irreplaceable, and his legacy of poems, essays, and plays a community treasure.

Franklin Abbott

*

I sensed soon after meeting Yves in 1980 that this multi-talented man was well on his way to a future filled with great things. How right I was. It became clear that his work, his performances, his persona were unique, ahead of their time in so many ways. What a magnificent man he was! Full of passion, power and grace. As I watched Assotto slip away on the day of his death I sensed that his legacy would grow and last for many years to come. How right I was.

Mace Anderson

*

When I think of the life of my cousin, Yves F. Lubin, I am overwhelmed with admiration. I am grateful to know that he cared, fought, gave, led, taught, encouraged, demonstrated, celebrated and loved. Because of his kindness, boldness and steadfastness, I rejoice. He dearly remains in my heart and I am so thankful for his life. Forever loved, Assotto Saint!

Always,
Guytele Lubin-Marsan and family

Acknowledgments

I am grateful to the following individuals, whose invaluable input and shared excitement helped make this book possible:

Mace Anderson, executor of Yves F. Lubin's estate, who is always there when needed. I thank him for his tremendous love, laughter, enthusiasm, and support in all of my decisions.

Walter Holland, who has always stood by my side as a great supporter of literary works, was extraordinarily helpful during the many stages of this book. He provided a wealth of knowledge, encouragement, and a memory that is as sharp as a knife, along with great editorial guidance.

Guytele Lubin-Marsan and Rachel Cassion Alerte, Yves' favorite cousins, provided additional childhood and family history that I am extremely grateful for. I am so happy that they can share in the celebration of their cousin's collected works.

Stephen Motika, publisher of Nightboat Books, who without hesitation expressed interest in publishing Assotto's works. He gave this book the wings it needed to fly. I am indebted to Lindsey Boldt and Gia Gonzales for the superb editorial guidance and all-around expertise. Their kindness, patience, and understanding can make any process easier. I am honored to work with Nightboat Books' incredible team. It indeed takes a village. I give profound thanks to Jaye Elizabeth Elijah, Rissa Hochberger, and Kit Schluter for their outstanding work.

Franklin Abbott and Jewelle Gomez who took the time to share their memories of Assotto and their knowledge of the gay Black writing community.

Pamela Sneed always freely offered her support, whether it was brainstorming about the book's title, reviewing history together, or writing the foreword. Her dedication to furthering Assotto's works is undeniable.

Jaime Shearn Coan's research, material aid, and his devotion to Assotto's works is heartening and I have deep gratitude for that. His amazing timeline of research and thought shows what true dedication is.

At the Schomburg Center for Research in Black Culture, the archivists in the Manuscripts, Archives and Rare Books Division; the Photographs and Prints Division; and the Moving Image and Recorded Sound Division are a pleasure to work with. I can't thank them enough for the handling of Assotto's works.

It takes a village and in all sincerity and gratitude I would like to thank Eric Washington, Becket Logan, Djola Branner, Philip Robinson, Cary Alan Johnson, Anthony Knight, André De Shields, Sarah Schulman, Stephen Booth, Robert Campbell, G. Winston James, Steve Langley, Rickey Butler, Blackberri, Allen Luther Wright, Reggie Harris, Bill (sic) Wright, Sur Rodney Sur, Steven G. Fullwood, Terence Taylor, Thomas Allen Harris, Jordan Schildcrout, PhD, and Jamez Smith.

345

Victoria Werner, my wife, the unofficial co-editor of Assotto's collected works, thank you for sharing the love of books. Thank you always for your unconditional love .

Assotto placed his own acknowledgments in the books he published. I have included those acknowledgments below:

Marie Lubin, Jan Holmgren, Pedro Perez, Phill Wilson, Vega, Marvin White, Arthur T. Wilson, Bil Wright, Leif Ahlgren, Mark Ameen, Maceo Anderson, Dennis Rager, Willie C. Barnes, Melvin Dixon, David Frechette, Carl Morse, Sean Drake, Rotimi Fani-Kayode, James Smith, Rodney Dildy, Akhenaton Charles, Mark Telzer, Charles Michael Smith, Thomas Harris, Jacquie Bishop, Blackberri, Michael Lassell, Michael Lee, Jim Marks, Al Meynet, Thomas Glave, Bradley S. Phillips, Don Reid, Marlon Riggs, Michael Shernoff, Rachel Cassion Alerte, Michele Karlsberg, Sapphire, Bree Scott-Hartland, David Trinidad, Phil Wilke, Aaron Woodruff, Other Countries, Redvers JeanMarie, Oye Apeji Ajanaku, Thom Bean, Mark Haile, Warren Bradley, Kenton Grey, Michael Cummings, Essex Hemphill, Craig G. Harris, Isaac Jackson, Joseph Long, Thomas Allen Harris, Gay Men Of African Descent, Men of All Colors Together, The Black Gay and Lesbian Leadership Forum, New York State Council of the Arts and his co-workers from the NYC Health and Hospitals Corporation.

In closing, I would be remiss not to acknowledge the over eighty-five million people infected with HIV around the world along with the over 40 million that have died from AIDS. Call their names.

Contributors

Yves François Lubin (aka Assotto Saint) was a Haitian-born American writer, performer, publisher, and AIDS activist. He heavily contributed to increasing the visibility of contemporary Black queerness in the cultural arts movement of the '80s and early '90s. Saint drew upon his Haitian heritage, music, incantations, and radical politics to weave together a tapestry of literature that celebrates life in the face of death, and embraces politics as a way to change the world. He served as a mentor to an entire generation of up-and-coming gay Black community members. As publisher of Galiens Press, Saint published two volumes of his own poetry, *Stations* and *Wishing For Wings*, and edited two seminal anthologies of gay Black writing: the 1991 Lambda Literary Award–winning *The Road Before Us: 100 Gay Black Poets* and *Here To Dare: 10 Gay Black Poets*. His chapbook *Triple Trouble* was published in Tongues Untied (GMP, London). He was also the author of such plays as *Risin' To The Love We Need*, *New Love Song*, *Black Fag*, and *Nuclear Lovers*. In 1990, he was awarded both the Fellowship in Poetry from the New York Foundation for the Arts and the James Baldwin Award from the Black Gay Leadership Forum. He lived in New York City with Jan Urban Holmgren, his life partner and co-founder of Metamorphosis Theater and the techno-pop band Xotika. Lubin died June 29, 1994 of AIDS-related complications.

Pamela Sneed is a New York-based poet, performer and visual artist.

Jaime Shearn Coan, PhD, is a writer living in Brooklyn, NY/ Lenapehoking, and is completing a monograph and digital archive on the performances and lifeworlds of Assotto Saint.

Michele Karlsberg is an award-winning publicist, producer, publisher, advocate, and author. She manages the estates of artists Assotto Saint, Roy Gonsalves, and Stan Leventhal, helping to keep their creative works available.

PHOTOGRAPHS

Front endpaper
Assotto Saint, New York City, 1989. Photograph by Alcindor.
© Estate of Yves F. Lubin.

Frontispiece
Assotto Saint, London, 1988. Photograph by Rotimi Fani-Kayode.
© Rotimi Fani-Kayode.

Page xii
Yves François Lubin, Les Cayes, Haiti. © Estate of Yves F. Lubin.

Page 2
Jan Urban Holmgren, New York City, New York.
© Estate of Yves F. Lubin

Page 4
Yves François Lubin, Queens, NY, March 1979. © Estate of Yves F. Lubin.

Page 16
Assotto Saint, Gold Headdress and Leather Flogger, New York City.
© Estate of Yves F. Lubin.

Page 30
Assotto Saint & Jan Urban Holmgren, New York City, 1988.
Photograph by Alcindor. © Estate of Yves F. Lubin.

Page 122
Assotto Saint and his mother Marie Myriam Lubin, March On
Washington, Washington, DC, 1993. © Estate of Yves F. Lubin.

Page 220
Assotto Saint, New York City. © Estate of Yves F. Lubin.

Page 328
Assotto Saint & Jan Urban Holmgren, HOP Rally, Union Square, New York
City, 1992. Photograph by Eric K. Washington. © Eric K. Washington.

Back endpaper
Assotto Saint, New York City, 1993. Photograph by Becket Logan.
© Becket Logan.

Nightboat Books

Nightboat Books, a nonprofit organization, seeks to develop audiences for writers whose work resists convention and transcends boundaries. We publish books rich with poignancy, intelligence, and risk. Please visit nightboat.org to learn about our titles and how you can support our future publications.

The following individuals have supported the publication of this book. We thank them for their generosity and commitment to the mission of Nightboat Books:

Kazim Ali • Anonymous (8) • Mary Armantrout • Jean C. Ballantyne • Thomas Ballantyne • Bill Bruns • John Cappetta • V. Shannon Clyne • Ulla Dydo Charitable Fund • Photios Giovanis • Amanda Greenberger • Vandana Khanna • Isaac Klausner • Shari Leinwand • Anne Marie Macari • Elizabeth Madans • Martha Melvoin • Caren Motika • Elizabeth Motika • The Leslie Scalapino - O Books Fund • Robin Shanus • Thomas Shardlow • Rebecca Shea • Ira Silverberg • Benjamin Taylor • David Wall • Jerrie Whitfield & Richard Motika • Arden Wohl • Issam Zineh

This book is made possible, in part, by grants from the New York City Department of Cultural Affairs in partnership with the City Council, the New York State Council on the Arts Literature Program, and the National Endowment for the Arts.